EASTERN PATHS AND
THE CHRISTIAN WAY

TO
CINDY AND CATHY

Whose Capacity to Live in Both
East and West
Keeps the Home Lively
and
All Questions Open

EASTERN PATHS AND THE CHRISTIAN WAY

Paul Clasper

ORBIS BOOKS

Maryknoll, New York 10545

The Catholic Foreign Mission Society of America (Maryknoll) recruits and trains people for overseas missionary service. Through Orbis Books Maryknoll aims to foster the international dialogue that is essential to mission. The books published, however, reflect the opinions of their authors and are not meant to represent the official position of the society.

Copyright © 1980 by Orbis Books, Maryknoll NY 10545

Manufactured in the United States of America

Library of Congress Cataloging in Publication Data

Clasper, Paul D
  Eastern paths and the Christian way.

  Includes bibliographies.
  1. Christianity and other religions—Hinduism.
2. Hinduism—Relations—Christianity. 3. Christianity and other religions—Buddhism. 4. Buddhism—Relations—Christianity. I. Title.
BR128.A77C55   261.2'4   80-13730
ISBN 0-88344-100-4 (pbk.)

CONTENTS

CHAPTER THREE:
THERAVADA BUDDHISM:
THE EIGHT-FOLD PATH TO
NIRVANA   33

CHAPTER FOUR:
ZEN: THE PATHLESS PATH TO
AUTHENTIC LIVING   48

1

THE ENCOUNTER
OF FAITHS TODAY

The Christian Way, at its best, has been a source of healthful, new life. It brings healing where there is dis-ease; integration where there is dis-integration; vision where there is blindness; vitality where there is sluggishness; freedom where there is enslavement; and above all, fellowship where there is loneliness.

But, from the start, the Christian Way has persisted in a world filled with many other Paths which also claim to lead to freedom and enlightenment. (The term "Way" was one of the earliest descriptions of the Christian movement. For convenience I will use it consistently for the Christian Way and use the term "Paths" for the time-honored Asian religious quests.) Our world continues to be filled with roads to salvation (meaning methods for gaining power to make whole, or healthful). Whether these Paths are all true, all false, all the same, or partially true and partially false is one of the gnawing questions of our time.

The Christian Way claims to be a (or *the*) message of "Good News" (Gospel). It points to an active, transforming source of good. But it never exists in a vacuum. It is surrounded by pessimists and also by many other bearers of good news. The pessimists say that the Christian Good News is mere wishful thinking; it is the illusion of those who cannot face the hard realities of life; it is the opium which keeps the faithful drugged. But there is also an endless stream of other good-news bearers. These are representatives of deeply insightful Paths, with roots deep in human experience, which seek to point the road from brokenness to health, from frustration to self-realization.

The various Asian Paths, or Asian religions, have always constituted a special challenge to the Christian Way. In a sense they are older than the Christian Way. But antiquity is not their strongest claim to respect. They have shown a persisting vitality; they are always being renewed. We are living in a time of remarkable resurgence and expansion of many of these well-trodden Asian Paths.

This book is concerned with a deeper, more sympathetic understanding of *both* the Christian Way and the Asian Paths. It is also concerned with the quality of the encounter that takes place when the Way and the Paths meet.

AMERICAN BUDDHISTS AND BURMESE BAPTISTS

A few years ago I was living in Burma and teaching in the Burma Divinity School, which is located on Seminary Hill, Insein, ten miles north of Rangoon. One day a neighbor, the sister of a faculty colleague, became ill and was taken to the Rangoon General Hospital. After a week she returned to the campus and came in to give me a report of her hospital experience.

She told me that during her hospitalization she had the most interesting roommate. She had been with a most likeable young American woman, roughly her own age, who had come to Asia to seriously study Buddhism. Before reaching Burma the American had visited several other Buddhist countries, spending time at various monasteries, pagodas, and sacred mountains. She had recently taken a Buddhist vow and was wearing the traditional robe of the Buddhist nun. In the course of staying in a local monastery she had picked up some intestinal trouble and had been rushed to the hospital.

My neighbor (who spoke English well) told me how exciting their conversation had been. The American girl shared with her why she had this deep interest in coming to Asia to study Buddhism. In turn the young Burmese woman had shared with the American the meaning of the Christian Way as she had experienced it in a Buddhist country. She suggested that the American was a bit lonely, spoke only English, and that sometime I might pay her a visit.

The next time I was in Rangoon I visited the enter-prising American student of Buddhism. I recall my amazement at seeing for the first time an American with her head completely shaved in the fashion of the Buddhist nun. By now she was feeling well again, and I remember the conversation with great pleasure. She was a college graduate with a long-standing interest in Asian religion and philosophy. She felt much affinity with Buddhism and wanted to experience it in the Asian context, not simply the American classroom. She impressed me as tolerant, genial, and questing. She had great respect for my Burmese Christian neighbor. We were able to share with each other something of the quests which had brought us both to Burma.

I have often thought of that week of conversation between those women in the hospital room in Rangoon. Perhaps it is a kind of parable of the new stage of the encounter of faiths in our time. The Burmese Baptist woman came from a solidly Christian home. Her brother was a professor in the Burman Theological Seminary and now serves as its president. Her father was a respected Christian pastor. Behind her were three generations of the Christian tradition dating back to Adoniram Judson, America's first Protestant missionary to Asia. Her family was well educated; her sisters were high-school teachers. She herself was a Sunday-school teacher who, among other things, taught Burmese dancing to American girls—my daughter being one of them! She gave every impression of being a rooted, attractive, knowledgeable Christian living in an Asian, Buddhist country.

The American seemed more unusual at the time. But in the decade since that conversation she seems far more typical of the current youth generation. I think of her now as something of the avant-garde of her generation. For the present appeal of Asian religion to the American youth generation is a new fact, a phenomenon unprecedented in our history. Thousands in our time in the West have become serious disciples of such disciplines as Theravada Buddhist meditation, Krishna worship, Kundalini Yoga, Zen, Tai Chi, and dozens of other Asian Paths.

In our time it is not simply Western Christians meeting Asian Buddhists. The times are far more exciting and the encounter far more demanding. Authentic Asian Christians are now meeting new, young, Western "seekers" or adherents of old-but-ever-renewed Asian Paths. (I make the assumption that the Christian Way is potentially universal and that the Asian Christians with whom I have lived and worked are as "authentically Christian" as those I have known in the West.) This situation calls for a deepening of our understanding: a deeper understanding of both *our* faith and the faiths by which *others* are seeking to live.

THE NEW IMPACT OF EAST ON WEST

Professor Arnold Toynbee, the eminent British historian, has speculated concerning the new stage of the meeting of East and West. His "long view," based on a vast knowledge of the movements of civilizations, is worth pondering. Some years ago he suggested that if we could look ahead to, say, the year 2047, we would see that the period leading up to this time had been characterized by the overwhelming impact of the West on the East. But the tide is already beginning to turn. If we could look ahead to, say, 3047 we would see that a reverse process had taken place. This coming period will be the time of the strong, though more subtle, impact of the East on the West. He dared to think that if we could imagine 4047 we would see the time of the unification of East and West in the *oikoumene,* in a one-world civilization. In that far-off unified world the insights of the religions of the East, he firmly believed, would be more deeply influential than the now dominant technology of the West.

In our generation such writings as *Future Shock* have led us to believe that the pendulum of change is moving much more rapidly than Toynbee might have expected. But the broad lines of his thesis are still worth pondering. There are many reasons to believe that we are in a time of the subsiding of the impact of West on East, though some of it will obviously continue. Perhaps in the response of the youth generation in the West (where we would expect changing currents to be felt) we are seeing the beginning stages of the subtle-but-pervasive countercurrent of the Eastern impact on the West. If so, the new interest in the Asian Paths must not be simply dismissed as the latest passing fad, which will soon evaporate like the morning mist. This *may* be the beginning of a movement which, in various forms, will characterize the new period into which we are just now moving.

FROM A PATCHWORK QUILT TO A PIECE OF SHOT-SILK

The religious map of the world is being rapidly changed. It is no longer true that the religions are in neat, carefully separated geographical blocks: Americans as Christians; Indians as Hindus; Burmese as Buddhists; Israelis as Jews; Indonesians as Islamists. Increasingly the Way is everywhere and all of the major Paths are everywhere. This fact makes new demands on our self-understanding and our understanding of our neighbors and the other Paths.

Toynbee has forecast this:

> In the next chapter [of history] we may expect to see all the now surviving faiths continue to hold the field side by side and continue to divide the allegiance of mankind between them. But we may also expect to see the individual's adherence to a particular faith determined, in an ever larger number of instances, not by the geographical accident of the locality of his birthplace, but by a deliberate choice of the faith with which

he feels closest personal affinity—a feeling that will, presumably, be determined by the type of his psychological organization and orientation. The adherents of each religion thus seem likely, in the next chapter, to come gradually to be distributed all over the *oikoumene* but it may be expected that, in the process, they will come to be intermingled everywhere with adherents of all the other faiths, as the Jews are intermingled with Muslims and Christians and the Parsees with Muslims and Hindus. As a result, the appearance of the religious map of the *oikoumene* may be expected to change from the pattern of a patchwork quilt to the texture of a piece of shot-silk.[1]

In *the time of the patchwork quilt* one's Path was, for the most part, already selected: we followed the Path of those on our block. Knowing "our" Path seemed quite sufficient. But in *the time of a piece of shot-silk* there is a great opportunity for choice and for confusion. In this time those who know only one Path really know no Path. We are forced to know by comparison. It is also possible to drift with no identity, which is the easiest way to become a nonentity. The Shot-Silk Era is far more demanding; we must make far more choices and we must have a more sensitive understanding of the many Paths.

THE CHRISTIAN WAY IN THE SHOT-SILK ERA

The demand for intelligent dialogue between the followers of the Way and the Asian Paths will seem frightening to many. The Shot-Silk Era will call for fresh, basic thinking; honest, comprehending listening; and genuine conversation (not lengthy monologues). The willingness to learn will be a precondition for the right to preach or teach. There is every reason to wince at these stern demands.

But the Community of the Resurrection (another name for the followers of the Way) has no reason to fear. This community has been in this situation before. Looking back, the times most like the Shot-Silk Era have been the times of the most imaginative missionary activity and the periods of creative theological construction.

Hendrik Kraemer, a missionary theologian who spent many years at the grassroots level of the Christian mission in Indonesia, has said: "In regard to the contemporary non-Christian religions, the main remark to be made in this context is that for the first time since the Constantine victory in A.D. 312 and its consequences, the Christian Church is heading towards a real and spiritual encounter with the great non-Christian religions. Not only because the so-called younger churches, the fruits of the work of modern missions, live in the midst of them, but also because the fast-growing interdependence of the whole world forces the existence and vitality of these religions upon us, and makes them a challenge to the Church to manifest in new terms its spiritual and intellectual integrity and value."[2]

Prior to A.D. 312 the struggling Christian community led a precarious and pilgrim existence in the midst of the numerous Eastern and Graeco-Roman Paths which filled the Mediterranean world. Frequently the Way was persecuted as a sect that seemed subversive to the interests of the Empire. Martyrs were plentiful; it was often risky to be a known follower of the Way. It was necessary to give reasons for choosing this Way.

This pressure gave birth to vigorous theology. In order to communicate the Christian faith the best interpreters borrowed freely from the language and customs of the nearby Paths. To move to the not-yet-known it was important to utilize the already known. The most effective interpreters were those who knew at least two languages: the language of one of the well-known Paths and the new language developing in the Community of the Resurrection. Followers of the Way readily baptized elements of the surrounding culture into their own life and mission.

But in 312, when the Emperor Constantine proclaimed Christianity as the established state religion, a whole new situation emerged. It became very respectable, and likely to one's economic advantage, to belong to the "Religion of the Establishment." This "culture religion" was only slightly related to the original ethos of the followers of the Way. From then until relatively recent times the Way has persisted under the protecting umbrella of the establishment known as "Western Christendom." At times this "protection" has almost meant the smothering of all that is vital. But the Way has persisted, as often "in spite of" Christendom as because of it.

The planting of new colonies of the Way in Asia and Africa, through the work of the modern missionary movement, produced many situations much like those of the early Church. Followers of the Way had to lead a struggling, risky, pilgrim existence in the face of the ancient Paths of India, Burma, Thailand, Vietnam, China, Japan, and Indonesia. But even this is not the whole story. For the beginning of these new communities of the Way also took place under the protecting umbrella of the Western colonial rule of England, France, and Holland.

Now this situation has abruptly changed. The increasingly secularizing forces in the West have pulled down the protecting umbrella of "Western Christendom." Religiously one can be anything or nothing in the West. Teachers of Krishna-consciousness, Buddhist meditation, and Tibetan mysticism move freely in Western cities and universities. In Asian countries the colonial umbrella has been ripped down. Asian Paths, with new dignity and aggressiveness, pursue missionary work in both East and West. The Christian Way, in both East and West, finds itself in a much more exposed and demanding encounter with the Asian Paths—more so than at any time since A.D.312.

It now seems self-evident that serious followers of the Way will need to understand not only their own Way, but the mind-set of both the pessimists who deny the validity of all Paths, and the various Paths which claim to lead from darkness to light and from bondage to freedom. Classes for instruction for serious membership in the Way will need to include some knowledge of the basic documents and root metaphors (Scripture) of the Movement, some history of the ongoing life of the Movement, and the principles and practice called for in today's mission. *But this in itself will not be sufficient.* A careful, honest presentation of some of the other Paths will also be necessary. When these are presented with sympathetic understanding there is always the risk that potential followers of the Way may change their minds and decide for another Path. This risk must be taken. If the other Paths are "put down" in a high-handed way (comparing our best with their worst!) this may very well become the reason for potential followers of the Way to give up on the Way, as if it were based on fear and dishonesty. On the other hand a careful, fair, and unfrantic comparison may turn out to be one of the most compelling reasons for embracing the Way. Integrity in dealing with the Way, the pessimists, and the other Paths must be the hall-mark of nurture and mission in the Shot-Silk Era.

THE PURPOSE AND PLAN OF THIS BOOK

My purpose in writing this book is to make some modest but solid contribution to the fruitfulness of the new encounter of faiths in our time. Any effort toward a deeper understanding of *both* the Way and the Asian Paths would seem like time well-spent. But what the results will be of a "more fruitful encounter" is hard to predict, and certainly impossible to control.

One result from such a study as this is to be saved (somewhat, at least) from the tendency toward glib generalizations. It will be less easy to chirp about the superiority of *my* faith over other faiths. It will also be less easy to glibly assert that all Paths are basically saying the same thing. But salvation from glibness is not easy; it leaves one with less to say and more to ponder. This may be good for us, but it is a costly good!

Another result from this study may be the realization that the communication of our faith is as difficult as the honest understanding of the other's. A new and very different sympathy for the world mission of the Christian community usually results from the effort to hear the other Paths at their best. Some long-time support for the Christian mission for the wrong reasons may well cease. On the other hand, some new support for the right reasons may begin to arise. (Often those committed to the support of the status quo of "Christian missions" are too busy to engage in trying to hear what other faiths have to say.)

It may turn out that the encounter with others' Paths may lead to a purging of some of the dross that has accumulated in my practice of the Way. This recognition would not be easy; we are prone to be defensive about being helped by followers of other Paths. But if it really did happen, we could be grateful for the purging. But what would happen if it worked the other way? Followers of other Paths might be purged by contact with the Way. If the Way made this contribution to the purging of the Paths, would we be glad or sorry? One thing is sure: an increase of understanding may not make life easier; but it will make it richer and more fruitful.

Once having made a case for the importance of the subject, my plan is to listen as attentively as possible to three of the most ancient, but currently most appealing, Asian Paths: Hinduism, Theravada Buddhism, and Zen. I have selected these three as typical examples of some of the best of the Asian Paths. I believe they have intrinsic importance because they have persisted for several thousand years. But, even more, they are among the most attractive voices heard in the West today. Hinduism, or "The Spiritual View of the Universe," has a way of always reappearing in various forms. It seems never to lose its appeal. Theravada, or "classical," Buddhism claims to be the authentic Path of the Buddha, who is called "The Light of Asia." In many ways this is the clearest, sharpest, most radical alternative to the Way. Zen claims to be the living heart of all religion, but not "just another religion." Its impact on the West in this generation has been phenomenal, especially in intellectual and artistic circles.

In the chapters devoted to each of these Paths I will largely reproduce what I have often heard dedicated exponents of these Paths say when invited to speak to Western inquirers. I claim no originality here. I have tried to reproduce faithfully what they have most wanted Western people to know about their Path.

My method is not to reproduce a mini-history of the Path in question. Rather, by means of stories, symbols, quotations, and descriptions I hope to unfold the central vision of each of these Paths. I hope by pointing to the center that "the rose will unfold." I do not intend to dissect the rose. I will aim at the most sympathetic understanding of the best of the Asian Paths. I do not want to simply pile up facts. My appeal will be to what Wordsworth called "the feeling intellect." A list of books for further reading follows each chapter.

Following this I will devote Chapter 5 to an interpretation of the Way. Since this book is primarily directed to those with some degree of understanding of the Way I will assume a larger familiarity with the Way than with the Asian Paths.

In Chapter 6 I will look at some of the models which have been used, and are still being used, in relating the Way to the Asian Paths. To understand these may help us either to refurbish some old models, or to get beyond the old to the construction of new models.

Chapter 7 will conclude with a description of the

"passing over" to another faith by sympathetic understanding and the "coming back," as the peculiar
spiritual adventure of our time. An awareness of this
may well be crucial, not only for understanding the
children in our own homes, but for making possible
the growth in the future which we so much need and
which the Creative Spirit is ever seeking to bring about
in our times.

JUSTIN MARTYR CONTINUES TO WEAR HIS BLUE ROBE

Among some Roman Catholics there is a tradition
that before embarking on a long journey it is wise to
invoke the help of a saint. Of course the Holy Spirit is
an ever-present source of strength. But the inspiration
of a fellow struggler who has modeled the life of courage and grace is also heartening. I think there is wisdom in this urge.

As I undertake this study I am especially conscious
of a second-century Church Father whose example
seems especially appropriate to our time—Justin,
characterized as "philosopher and martyr." His early
life was spent as a conscientious teacher of the best of
Greek wisdom. He wore the celebrated blue robe of
the teacher of philosophy. In his quest for insight and
fullness of life he had traveled through most of the
Paths of religion and philosophy of his time. But one
day during a solitary walk by the seashore he encountered "a venerable old Christian of pleasant counte-
nance and gentle dignity" who began to unfold quietly
the biblical faith of the Hebrew prophets and the
"*Logos* (Word or Truth) made flesh in Jesus Christ." In
time this vision of the Way transformed his life and he
became an interpreter of the Christian faith to the

inquirers of his time. But, having become a Christian, he now wondered if he should discard the blue robe that symbolized a noble profession dedicated to understanding the best of the Greek heritage. He decided not to discard the robe. He believed that the fullness of life he had come to know through the Christ (the *Logos*) did not negate, but rather completed, the best he had seen around him. In fact, he now saw the previous Paths in a wholly new light. He saw them both more critically and with an enlarged understanding and perspective.

Since the Christ was the *Logos* (Word of God), he saw "sperms of the *Logos*" scattered throughout the best of the religious and philosophical Paths in his world. He wrote: "Those who live according to the *Logos* are Christians, even though they are accounted atheists. Such were Socrates and Heroditus among the Greeks. . . . Whatever has been uttered aright by any man in any place belongs to us Christians; for, next to God, we worship and love the *Logos* which is from the unbegotten and ineffable God. . . . For all the authors were able to see the truth darkly through the implanted seed of the *Logos* dwelling in them."[3]

He has left the example of a life totally dedicated to interpreting the Way at a critical period in history. While never sentimental or uncritical, he had the largest possible appreciation for the cultural heritage about him. He was concerned to see the Way in relationship to the existing Paths. In time he sealed his work and testimony with his own blood.

Seeing that we are surrounded by a host of witnesses (martyrs) such as Justin, we can find courage for the venture of understanding that our times require.

NOTES

1. Arnold Toynbee, *An Historian's Approach to Religion,* Gifford Lecture Series (London: Oxford University Press, 1956), pp. 138–139.

2. Hendrik Kraemer, *Religion and the Christian Faith* (Philadelphia: Westminster, 1957), p. 20.

3. Justin, *Apology* I, xlvi–II, xiii, quoted in Henry Bettenson, comp. and ed., *Documents of the Christian Church* (London: Oxford University Press, 1963; rev. ed. 1970), pp. 8–9.

Suggestions for Further Reading

Cragg, Kenneth. *Christianity in World Perspective.* London: Oxford, 1968.

Forman, Charles W. *A Faith for the Nations.* Layman's Theological Library. Philadelphia: Westminster, 1957.

Kraemer, Hendrik. *World Cultures and World Religions.* Philadelphia: Westminster, 1960.

Tillich, Paul J. *Christianity and the Encounter of World Religions.* New York: Columbia University Press, 1963.

Toynbee, Arnold J. *Christianity among the Religions of the World.* New York: Scribners, 1957.

2

HINDUISM: MANY PATHS
LEAD TO REALITY

Hinduism may well claim to be the oldest, the most persistent, the most flexible, and the most alluring of the many Asian Paths. Actually, it is better to think of it as a composite of many Paths, all of which can lead to reality, God, deliverance, or self-realization. Hinduism is "the Perennial Philosophy"; the timeless "Spiritual View of the Universe." It never really disappears from the scene. It takes on new forms in new ages and in various cultures. The Way has always had to encounter forms of this under many names. Likely this is the most *subtle* challenge which the Way faces.

THE UNIVERSAL PRAYER

The Hindu believes there is a common, underlying unity to all of the religious quests for self-realization. If we can accentuate what we have in common, and not make too much of incidental differences, we will be well on our way to a deeper understanding and a more mature human experience.

One of the oldest recorded prayers is found in the

Hindu Scriptures known as the *Upanishads*. If we can all pray this prayer together there is every reason to feel we have the deepest things in common. Praying and worshipping together would seem to be the finest way of gaining an understanding of the Hindu Path, or Paths. The prayer is:

> From unreality lead us to reality
> From darkness lead us to light
> From bondage lead us to freedom[1]

The Hindu feels that this prayer can be a vehicle for expressing our deepest yearning. If this is so we are well on our way to understanding Hinduism, and making the discovery that in our deepest needs and quests we are one people.

Our deepest drive is for freedom from all that binds us, light for our dark way, and a sense of reality instead of the superficial and phony which seem to dominate us. But why do we all, regardless of time or country, desire this fulfillment? This very prayer within us is evidence of the indwelling Spirit of Truth (or "God," if we choose to use this word) breathing through us, and in so doing drawing us to freedom, light, and the really real.

One of the key words for the Hindu is *Moksha*—deliverance. We long with deep yearning for emancipation from the enslaving powers that operate without and within. The multiple Hindu Paths are ways to achieve this liberation. Enlightenment and liberation will be, again and again, the themes of the Asian Paths.

THE GOAL OF THE HUMAN QUEST

The Westminster Catechism opens with a succinct statement of the goal for humanity by saying that "man's chief end is to glorify God, and to enjoy him forever." A somewhat similar, succinct statement of the Hindu goal of life can be found in the *Bhagavad-Gita,* the most popular and influential of all Hindu writings. (Actually the *Gita* is not in the official canon of Scripture, but it is called, "The Layman's Upanishad." It is by any standard one of the world's best loved and most influential books.) The ultimate Spirit, or God, speaks:

> He who is free from delusion, and knows me as the Supreme Reality, knows all that can be known. Therefore he adores me with his whole heart. This is the most sacred of all the truths I have taught you. He who has realized it becomes truly wise. The purpose of his life is fulfilled.[2]

Here the basic themes of the Hindu Path are set forth in classical simplicity. We are meant for fulfillment. But the realization of our potential is also at the same time the divine Self-realization in and through us. The unity of our small life with the source of universal life is the simplest and deepest truth to be known.

To *know* God, or the supreme reality, is to *adore* "It," or "Life," or "God," or "Him," or "Her." This *knowing* is not the accumulation of facts or the precise descriptions with which science deals. To *know* God is to *"realize"* the unity of life with its source. This knowledge becomes *wisdom,* which is a quality that infuses all of life.

THE ONE REALITY (GOD) IS CALLED BY MANY NAMES

Already it has been observed that the Hindu prefers to use a variety of terms for—for what? What shall we

call the source of life? In one of the oldest of the
Hindu Scriptures, the Rig Veda, there is this famous
text:

> They call him Indra, Mitra, Varuna, Agni; and he is
> the heavenly noble-winged Garutman.
> To what is one, sages give many a title: they call it
> Agni, Yama, Matarusvan.[3]

The sages are exceedingly verbal! They seek to clas-
sify, or point, by means of words and names. But each
word limits as well as hints. A word or name can indi-
cate an aspect of the divine life. God is light, or power,
or truth, or love. God is like a shepherd who cares, or a
potter who shapes clay, or a judge who gives verdicts.
All analogies have a certain validity; but each has distinct limitations which can easily distort the whole picture. Many words are needed. It is safer to use many
rather than distort the ultimate by a too narrow or
limited selection of analogies.

For Hindus the favorite term for the supreme
ultimate is *Brahman.* But this sole source is best known
through a trinity of self-revelation. *Brahman* is also
known as *Brahma*—the creator; *Vishnu*—the preserver;
and *Shiva*—the destroyer (or, the energy which breaks
up in order to re-create). The most popular aspects of
the divine for worship and devotion are *Vishnu* and
Shiva, or the love and the power of the eternal Spirit.
But *Vishnu* and *Shiva* in turn have many aspects and
names. "To what is one, the sages have given many
names." But the worship of any aspect is actually a
worship of the sole source.

It can be seen that the Hindu has a preference for
what could be called the more "impersonal" analogies
or names. These seem to the Hindu to be more re-

spectful. But the more intimate and personal terms are also used by those who particularly find them congenial.

But beyond all words silence is prized. Words are not to be despised; but the Hindu responds to the wisdom which says: "In the face of the ultimate, a respectful silence is the best posture."

THE BLIND PRIESTS AND THE ELEPHANT

A story that every Hindu child learns early unfolds the very heart of this vision of reality.

Once there were three blind priests (Brahmins). They stood feeling a large elephant and shouting their descriptions to each other. The first said, "It is like a cement wall; rough and flat." He was feeling the side. The second said, "No! It is like a rope. I am swinging back and forth on it." He was holding the trunk. The third said, "You foolish old men! You are both wrong. It is like a tree trunk. I can reach around it." He was encircling the elephant's leg.

Once this story is "seen" few words are necessary! All descriptions of the boundless Life are right, as far as they go. But they are limited to such a small grasp. Even the combination of all descriptions would be far short of the many-sided, richly living reality of the Life-Giver.

The limitations of our grasp are not to be despised. But to claim that our simple view tells it all is the worst form of narrow-mindedness. This leads to intolerance, one of the worst forms of evil. The Hindu seeks to cultivate an appreciation for diverse names, descriptions, and methods for self-realization. The divine is far greater than our little, blind groupings.

MANY PATHS LEAD TO *MOKSHA* (SALVATION)

Just as there are many names for the One-Beyond-All-Names, so there are many paths that can be traveled which will lead to enlightenment and liberation. The Hindus were fond of saying that there are as many paths as there are people.

But in the course of time three broad types of paths were emphasized. These, interestingly, turned out to correspond to the rough classification of people into basically thinkers, doers, and lovers. To be sure, one person may utilize more than one path. Ideally, the fully-orbed person would include all three elements in fruitful tension. But always the Hindu genius has been to see the underlying unity of these seemingly separate paths.

Hindus have always given a kind of highest priority to the thinkers. "The Way of the Intellect," or "The Path of the Philosophers," is called *Jnana Marga*. This is the way to union with God through knowledge. Understandably, this way is not open to all. But those with keen intellect can come to a vision of the essential unity of all life. "The Great Spirit (*Brahman*) and the human spirit (*Atman*) are one." We are, at our deepest, sparks from the eternal fire. All rivers flow to the ocean; we are, at best, drops which rightfully merge with the ocean of being.

But from the earliest times a path was recognized for those whose chief expression was in action rather than contemplation. The *Gita* states: "I have already told you that, in this world, aspirants may find enlightenment by two different paths. For the contemplative is the path of knowledge; for the active is the path of selfless action."[4]

THE PATH OF ACTION

Some of the finest passages in the *Gita* are descriptions of the path to God and self-realization through the faithful doing of one's duty. This is called *Karma Marga*. In our doing we are expressing the power of the divine life through us. This makes actions sacramental; our work is at the same time our worship. This is one path to union with *Brahman*. It is best to hear the actual words of the *Gita:*

> You have the right to work, but for the work's sake only. You have no right to the fruits of work. Desire for the fruits of work must never be your motive in working. Never give way to laziness, either.
>
> Perform every action with your heart fixed on the Supreme Lord. Renounce attachment to the fruits. Be even-tempered in success and failure; for it is evenness of temper which is meant by yoga.
>
> Work done with anxiety about results is far inferior to work done without such anxiety in the calm of self-surrender. Seek refuge in the knowledge of Brahman. They who work selfishly for results are miserable.
>
> Devote yourself, therefore, to reaching union with the *Brahman.* To unite the heart with *Brahman* and then to act; that is the secret of non-attached work. In the calm of self-surrender, the seers renounce the fruit of their actions, and so reach enlightenment.[5]

"The world is imprisoned in its own activity, except when actions are performed as worship of God. Therefore you must perform every action sacramentally, and be free from all attachments to results."[6]

This is the path of action freed from the sweaty compulsion of activism. It is the way of duty for duty's sake; not for personal advantage. The Hindu could say it means doing what we are called to do heartily, as unto God, not as a way of pleasing people.

THE PATH OF DEVOTION

But the chief contribution of the *Gita* was to stress a third path, beyond the two well-known paths of contemplation and action. This new emphasis was on the path of loving devotion, or self-surrender, as the path to union with God. This was called *Bhakti Marga.* This, in time, became one of the foremost paths; again and again this path produced saints and movements of spiritual renewal in Hinduism.

It is this insight into the response of love to the Great Lover which has endeared the *Gita* to the multitudes in India; this is also the reason for its present appeal to the West. Here are some of the favorite expressions:

> He who dwells
> United with Brahman,
> Calm in mind,
> Not grieving, not craving,
> Regarding all men
> With equal acceptance:
> He loves me most dearly.

Mentally resign all your action to me. Regard me as your dearest loved one. Know me to be your only refuge. Be united always in heart and consciousness with me.

United with me you shall overcome all difficulties by my grace.[7]

When the final climax of the book is reached there is

an appeal, as from the Life-Giver-and-Lover speaking to us all:

> Give me your whole heart
> Love and adore me,
> Worship me always
> Bow to me only
> And you shall find me:
> This is my promise
> Who love you dearly.
> Lay down all duties
> In me, your refuge.
> Fear no longer,
> For I will save you
> From sin and from bondage.[8]

RABINDRANATH TAGORE: POET OF MODERN HINDUISM

The *Gita* was written about the same time as the New Testament. It has continued to "speak" across the centuries and across cultures. Many of the same accents can be heard in a thoroughly modern poet such as Rabindranath Tagore. For many in the West Tagore is the best door into the heart of the Hindu perspective.

The path of action as a way to union with God, in contrast to sterile religious ritual, is described in this prose-poem from his famous collection known as *Gitanjali*:

> Leave this chanting and singing and telling of beads! Who doest thou worship in this lonely dark corner of a temple with doors shut? Open thine eyes and see thy God is not before thee!
>
> He is there where the tiller is tilling the hard ground and where the pathmaker is breaking stones. He is

with them in sun and in shower, and his garment is covered with dust. Put off thy holy mantle and even like him come down on the dusty soil!

Deliverance? Where is this deliverance to be found? Our master himself has joyfully taken upon him the bonds of creation; he is bound with us all forever.

Come out of thy meditations and leave aside thy flowers and incense! What harm is there if thy clothes become tattered and stained? Meet him and stand by him in the toil and the sweat of thy brow.[9]

The need to meet the divine love through self-surrender has been depicted forcefully in the following poem-parable:

I had gone a-begging from door to door in the village path, when thy golden chariot appeared in the distance like a gorgeous dream and I wondered who was this King of all kings!

My hopes rose high and me thought my evil days were at an end, and I stood waiting for alms to be given unasked and for wealth scattered on all sides in the dust.

The Chariot stopped where I stood. Thy glance fell on me and thou camest down with a smile. I felt that the luck of my life had come at last. Then of a sudden thou didst hold out thy right hand and say, "What hast thou to give me?"

Ah, what a kingly jest it was to open thy palm to a beggar to beg! I was confused and stood undecided, and then from my wallet I slowly took out the least little grain of corn and gave it to thee.

But how great was my surprise when at the day's end I empted the bag on the floor to find a least little grain of gold among the poor heap. I bitterly wept and wished that I had had the heart to give thee my all.[10]

Tagore is often described as one of the most "universal" men to appear in history. He is a kind of model of the meeting of East and West. He has embodied and synthesized in one life so many divergent strands. Yet his accents, which often sound so familiar to Western Christians, are deeply rooted in authentic Hindu spirituality. His description of *Vishnu*'s initiating love is an example of this.

> Have you not heard his silent steps? He comes, comes, ever comes. Every moment and every age, every day and every night he comes, comes, ever comes.
>
> Many a song have I sung in many a mood of mind, but all their notes have always proclaimed, "He comes, comes, ever comes."
>
> In the fragrant days of sunny April through the forest path, he comes, comes, ever comes.
>
> In the rainy gloom of July nights on the thundering chariot of clouds he comes, comes, ever comes.
>
> In sorrow after sorrow it is his steps that press upon my heart, and it is the golden touch of his feet that makes my joy to shine.[11]

LOVE'S MANY INCARNATIONS

One of the high peaks of Hindu insight is the sense of Love becoming incarnate again and again in order to bring aid to struggling people. Vishnu, the preserving-strengthening-unifying aspect of the divine, takes form in numerous *Avatars* (incarnations). Some say there have been a thousand incarnations; but the exact count is unimportant. Traditionally ten have been singled out for special recognition.

Among these embodiments is Rama, who, with his wife Sita, is worshipped as the example of tender and faithful family love. Perhaps the most frequently worshipped *Avatar* is Krishna. He is the voice of wisdom calling for devotion in the *Gita*. One form of the Krishna cult has recently become familiar on the streets of Western cities. To praise the power of Krishna is to seek to live by the power of the love that radiates through the universe.

Hindus are quick to believe that the power of compassion has been embodied in religious figures in other traditions. The Lord Buddha, for instance, is now considered one of the ten *Avatars* of Vishnu. Hindus believe that millions in Asia who do not call upon the name Krishna come to the knowledge of the truth (*Dharma*) through the life and teachings of the Buddha.

Most informed Hindus would like to include Jesus Christ, also, as the *Avatar* through whom most Western people have learned the truth about the power of love at the center of the universe. They would feel that it is quite incidental whether people pray to Krishna or to Christ. What is important is to pray, and to know that Love never wearies of coming to help in times of need.

There is also the expectation of coming *Avatars*. Where there is life there is love, which means hope. "He comes, comes, ever comes."

ONE TREE WITH MANY BRANCHES

The Hindu viewpoint is generous in its appreciation of the many paths that lead to *Moksha*—deliverance. This broad tolerance is possible because of the belief in the essential oneness of all the diverse paths.

A favorite figure for the essential unity of religions is that of the large tree, with roots deep in the soil and its widely extended branches. This giant tree draws from the rich soil of human experience; it is nourished by the sun, the wind, and the rain of the divine Spirit. The trunk is strong; the large branches reach out and eventually divide into smaller branches. New shoots and leaves come in their seasons.

The larger branches are the major religions such as Hinduism, Buddhism, Taoism, Christianity, and Islam. Large branches like Christianity divide again into branches such as Roman Catholicism, Eastern Orthodoxy, and Protestantism. The last again continually subdivides. But all of these, says the Hindu, are drawing from the same source. Religious differences are due to such factors as climates, culture, politics, and psychology.

It is not surprising that similar phenomena can be found in all of the branches of religion. Prayer, meditation, the reading of selected Scriptures, special festival days, the lives of saints and reformers, and the place of priests and teachers are part of the common religious heritage. Much can be learned from other traditions! But there is little point in trying to "convert" a person from one branch to another. Hindus are not trying to make Hindus out of Christians and Buddhists! Rather the Hindu seeks to deepen whatever religious life exists in any person; he knows that at the deepest levels all are nourished by the same source.

THE HINDU TEMPLE WELCOMES ONE MORE SYMBOL

When I lived in Rangoon, Burma, I frequently took visitors on a tour of some of the religious shrines in the city. I included a small, quiet Hindu temple just off one of the main streets. The priest of this temple was a friendly, obliging man who carefully interpreted his faith in good English to my tourist friends, who were largely American Christians.

His temple was less ornate and cluttered than many. The few images that he had were well selected and well placed on the walls of the central worship area. Vishnu and Shiva were there along with a few others. On one wall he had a fine image of the Buddha because, as he said, "Most people in this Buddhist country come to a knowledge of the truth through Gautama the Buddha."

But one wall was still empty. He would conclude his presentation by saying that he would really like to complete his temple by having some Christian symbol on that vacant wall. Then he would feel that all of the major religions were represented in his temple. He said that it would be easy enough to go out and purchase one, but it would mean much more to him if some Christian would care to contribute a Christian symbol as an indication of their desire for tolerance and better understanding between the faiths. He said that he was sure that most people in the West came to know God through Christ, even as Krishna was the path for many in India. He would conclude by saying that he hoped no narrowminded prejudice would keep some Christian from contributing a Christian symbol to his temple.

At this point my tourist friends would begin to fidget, look at their watches, express appreciation for the time he had given them, and look longingly for me to lead them on to the next pagoda!

What would you have done under these circumstances, and why?

NOTES

1. *Brihadaranvaka Upanishad.*
2. *Bhagavad-Gita: Song of God,* trans. Swami Prabhavananda and Christopher Isherwood, Mentor Religious Classics (New York: New American Library: 3rd ed. Cohasset, Mass.: Vedanta Centre, 1972), p. 113.
3. *Rig Veda,* I: 164, p. 46.
4. *Gita,* p. 44.
5. Ibid., pp. 40–41.
6. Ibid., p. 45.
7. Ibid., pp. 128–129.
8. Ibid., p. 129.
9. Rabindranath Tagore, *Gitanjali* (New York: Macmillan, 1971), p. 11.
10. Ibid., p. 40
11. Ibid., p. 47.

Suggestions for Further Reading

The Bhagavad-Gita, Mentor; many other editions available.

Prabhavananda, Swami. *The Spiritual Heritage of India.* New York: Doubleday, 1963; Hollywood: Vedanta Press.

Radhadkrishnan, Sarvapali. *The Hindu View of Life.* New York: Macmillan, 1939, 1962.

Ross, Nancy R. *Three Ways of Asian Wisdom: Hinduism, Buddhism, Zen, and Their Significance for the West.* New York: Simon and Schuster, 1937, 1966; Millwood, N.Y.: Kraus Reprint.

Smith, Huston. *The Religions of Man.* New York: Harper & Row, 1958, 1965.

Tagore, Rabindranath. *Gitanjali.* New York: Macmillan, 1971.

3

THERAVADA BUDDHISM: THE EIGHT-FOLD PATH TO NIRVANA

One of the most typical and influential of the Asian Paths is the Eight-Fold Path of Theravada Buddhism. The word "Theravada" means "The Way of the Elders." This is the school of Buddhism that claims to have preserved the original teachings and practices of the Lord Buddha with pristine purity. This is the "classical" school known also as the "southern school." It thrives today in Sri Lanka (Ceylon), Burma, Thailand, Cambodia, and Laos.

The Path is foundational for all other sects of Buddhism, such as the "northern school," or "Mahayana" tradition, found in China, Korea, and Japan. The term "Mahayana" means the "Large Vehicle," capable of adapting to various cultures and philosophies, and broad enough to include all types and conditions of people in the Buddhist Path. Theravada Buddhists see Mahayanists as hopelessly confused and compromised. They claim their Path to be the authentic way of the Lord Buddha.

Theravada Buddhism has endured for 2,500 years. In recent days it has experienced a great renewal of its vitality and missionary impulse. For many reasons, partly because of its rigor and austerity, it has had less appeal in the West. But it remains intrinsically important in its own right as one of the greatest of the Asian Paths. Not only is it highly influential in Asia; it also represents perhaps the sharpest alternative to the Christian Way. Here is one of the most consistent and persistent Asian Paths, which makes no claim to revelation, miracles, or the need for divine compassion. Whether there is a God or not is of no great importance. This, for the Theravadan, is a speculative question, and only diverts us from the ethical questions that we can deal with here and now. Ultimately even the existence of a "self" which knows is denied. Modern Theravada Buddhists believe their Path is peculiarly adapted to the scientific mentality; it deals only with phenomena that can be treated by the senses. Its meditation methods have been used by followers of all the major paths.

The closest Theravada Buddhism comes to a creed is the well-known Triple Gem. Followers of the Path affirm:

I take refuge in the Buddha
I take refuge in the Dhamma (the Truth, the Teaching)
I take refuge in the Sangha (the order of Monks, existing continuously since the time of the Lord Buddha)

This chapter will concentrate especially on the personality of the Lord Buddha and his basic teachings regarding the Eight-Fold Path to Nirvana.

THE LIFE OF THE BUDDHA

By any reckoning Gautama, the Buddha, is one of the most influential persons in history. Karl Jaspers, the German philosopher, began his monumental study *The Great Philosophers* by describing what he called the four "Paradigmatic Individuals." These are the foundational persons upon whom all subsequent thinking depends. He lists Buddha, Confucius, Socrates, and Jesus Christ.[1]

The Buddha is often called "The Light of Asia." His influence for 2,500 years on the vision and values of Asia is beyond calculation. Images of the Buddha dot the countryside throughout much of Asia; they are found in shrines in millions of homes. The Buddha continues to inspire courage and heroism where his path has been taken seriously. For "classical" Buddhism the memory of the events of the life of the Buddha is of utmost importance.

Gautama was born about 560 B.C. in northern India, about a hundred miles north of Benares. His father was king of a small kingdom. As a boy he was given every possible educational and cultural advantage. His father sensed that Gautama was a son of special destiny; consequently he did all he could to protect him from the outside world. Gautama grew up as a brilliant but over-protected aristocrat.

Near the age of thirty his complacency was shattered by a chance visit to the outside world. In quick succession he met an old man, a sick man, and a dead man. Like a flash he saw life's inevitable and irresistible drift toward old age, sickness, and death. Sensing that a pervasive suffering lay undisguised beneath the thin veneer of daily life, he determined to seek some solution to the problem of life's inescapable drift toward decay.

He then met a wandering monk, of whom there were many at the time. The youth movement of his day was on a passionate quest for some alternative to the suffering, superficial existence of the masses; the blatant hypocrisy of the "establishment"; and the superstition and vacuity of the priest-dominated religion. Many were on various quests or "trips" to discover new meaning and new styles of life. Gautama left home and joined the "seekers" of his generation by becoming a wandering monk.

For a few years he followed the religious paths current in India then and now. He gave himself to extreme ascetic practices, denying his body in order to enhance his spirit. But this did not satisfy. He gave himself to the disciplined study of all the philosophies of his time. After pursuing this to a dead-end he felt the "head trip" was wholly futile. In near despair, but with dogged perseverance, he went to the Bo-tree (an outdoor place for worship and meditation) and decided to wait until some light broke.

In time the light came. Gautama became the "Buddha," which means "The Enlightened One." The many pieces fell together with compelling clarity. He could now "see" what before had been only confusion. At first he was uncertain whether his new understandings could be preached with any effectiveness. He was tempted to pass immediately into the state of Nirvana (Peace) and not return to the decaying world. Eventually he resisted this temptation and began to preach the Truth *(Dhamma)* as he had discovered it.

He was predominately the teacher. He spoke with honesty, clarity, and compassion for all who would hear. Disciples began to flock to him. This was a threat to the religious establishment of his time. His teaching was called one of the great heresies. But he persisted during the next forty years. His time was largely divided between the popular teaching for the masses and the organization and deeper instruction of the monks. He lived to the ripe age of eighty, dying surrounded by many monks about the year 480 B.C.

THE FOUR NOBLE TRUTHS

What was the vision of truth that transformed Gautama, prince and monk, into the Buddha? Can this vision be communicated in sober prose?

From the first sermon of the Buddha to his very last words there is a remarkable, straightforward consistency in what he taught. He believed he had discovered the Truth *(Dhamma)* which had been given to seekers from age to age, but which always needed to be rediscovered and freshly taught.

This truth consisted in wisdom for life, which could be gained by a careful analysis of our experience. He likened himself to a practical physician. The first task was to recognize the disease and its seriousness; then one must understand the cause of the disease; finally one should prescribe the remedy. This analysis and prescription are found in the Four Noble Truths.

The First Noble Truth is the vivid awareness of the frustration and sense of unfulfillment that pervades all life. This has frequently been translated as "suffering."

Below even the most pleasant surface of life is deep trouble, restlessness, forces of decay and disintegration. To fail to acknowledge this seriously and personally is to be doomed to an illusory existence that is really a living death.

The Second Noble Truth is to see the cause of frustration, which is the passionate attempt to grasp and hold that which in the nature of the case is fleeting. We seek to possess; and the more we possess the more insatiable we become in our grasping. Whatever we try to possess and hold turns rancid or slips away. We desperately seek security; but change and insecurity is the essence of life. Our passion for attachment is the source of our dis-ease.

The Third Noble Truth is to determine to bring an end to this craving, grasping passion to clutch and hold.

The Fourth Noble Truth is the exposition of the Path that leads from the quagmire of passion, illusion, greed, and idolatry to the Nirvana of peace, light, and freedom. The Fourth Noble Truth is the Buddha's Eight-Fold Path.

THE EIGHT-FOLD PATH

The Buddha's path to Nirvana seems remarkably businesslike and uncomplicated. He saw it always as the "Middle Way" between violent and strained extremes. Extreme worldly attachment must be avoided; but so also should we avoid excessively complicated religious ritual and practices. The Middle Way was a sane, practical Path which all serious people could begin to follow, if they desired to move from a life of illusion and bondage to reality and freedom. The elements of the Path include the following:

1. *Right Knowledge.* The truth for life can be known. It is especially enshrined in the Four Noble Truths of the *Dhamma*.

2. *Right Aspiration.* There must be a serious and determined intent to shun the frivolous and follow the Path.

3. *Right Speech.* Gossip, idle chatter, and double-talk must be renounced. Careful, clean, and charitable language must be cultivated.

4. *Right Behavior.* Selflessness and courtesy must govern our actions. There must be no killing, stealing, lying, drinking of intoxicants, or unchastity.

5. *Right Livelihood.* Some occupations further the good life, while others keep one all day and every day clogged with poison.

6. *Right Effort.* Both sluggishness and frantic zeal are to be avoided. We must discover our own rhythm and steadily move at our own pace.

7. *Right Mindfulness.* To move ahead in the Path it is necessary to cultivate a careful analysis of life; an alert attentiveness to people and issues; a disciplined memory for recalling wise insights.

8. *Right Meditation.* The most developed and proven methods of yoga must be learned. These lead to self-control and mind-control which enable one to make progress in the Path.

The elements of the Eight-Fold Path can be regrouped to show more clearly the logic and direction of the Buddha's Path.

1. *Morality (Sila).* This includes elements 3, 4, 5, and 6. The Buddha begins by calling people to start *acting*. The frequent tendency, especially in religious matters, is to start speculating and to keep talking, arguing, and

comparing. This is futile. Even discussions about the existence or nonexistence of God can become a substitute for doing what now most needs to be *done*. Words can produce a verbal fog; what is called for is a decision and a single step in the right direction. Certain things must *not* be done; other good practices can be slowly and steadily learned. The Path to Nirvana begins with ethical seriousness, the accepting of personal responsibility, and the shunning of fruitless speculation and arguments.

2. *Meditation (Samadhi)*. This includes elements 7 and 8. In the course of time meditation techniques were developed with the exactness of a science. These included training for focusing the mind; achieving "one-pointedness"; lengthening periods of concentration; and contemplating those truths which strengthen one for the Path. Among the special themes for meditation was the "flowing," impermanent aspect of life. Monasteries were often located near rivers or flowing streams to enable this theme for meditation. The virtues of compassion and equanimity (steadiness of spirit, evenness of temper) were frequently objects of reflection. But meditation was never treated as an end in itself; it was a means or method for pursuing the Path.

3. *Wisdom (Panna)*. This includes elements 1 and 2. The achievement of wisdom is the goal of the Path. Wisdom means that ripe, mature seeing which issues in wholeness and fruition. It is enlightened freedom which is interfused with compassion.

NIRVANA

The Eight-Fold Path is a process which leads from bondage and illusion to Nirvana. But can Nirvana

really be described? Asian people have generally pre-
ferred "negative" descriptions; telling what it is not.
But this means they allow what it *is* to emerge without
an overload of heavy definitions or restricting
analogies. This positive use of negative description has
frequently led to the Western misunderstanding
that Nirvana is simply "nothingness" and "annihilation."

On this delicate subject the better part of wisdom
would be to let one of the most respected Buddhist
monks interpret in his own words what he believes
Nirvana to be. In recent years U Thittila, of Burma,
has been considered one of the best interpreters of
Theravada Buddhism to Western audiences. He describes Nirvana in this way:

> The predominance of the negative explanations of
> Nibbana [another expression for Nirvana] resulted in
> the mistaken notion that it is "nothingness" or "annihi-
> lation." However in the Pitakes [Theravada Buddhist
> Scriptures] we find many positive definitions of Nib-
> bana, such as Highest Refuge, Safety, Unique, Abso-
> lute Purity, Supramundane, Security, Emancipation,
> Peace, and the like. Nibbana is therefore not a negative
> concept because it is the cessation of craving, a "blow-
> ing out," for it is a blowing out of man's desires, and
> that blowing out of desires leaves a man free. Nibbana
> is freedom, but not freedom from circumstances; it is
> freedom from the bonds with which we have bound
> ourselves to circumstances. That man is free who is
> strong enough to say, "Whatever comes I accept as
> best.". . . Freedom means that one cannot be made a
> slave to anyone or anything because one is free from
> personal desire, free from resentment, anger, pride,
> fear, impatience—free from all craving. Such a man's
> binding emotions have been blown out like so many

candles. That man is free here on earth. He has reached Nibbana in this world.[2]

NO GOD, NO GRACE, NO PRAYER

In the classical Buddhist tradition the Buddha is a great teacher, but not a divine savior. On the question of the existence of God the Buddha chose to be a reverent agnostic; he said that he did not know and therefore would refrain from dogmatic statements. His stress was always on the actions that we can do now.

There is an austerity about the Buddha's Path. There are no ministering angels; there is no fund of stored up "grace," or reserve power, which one can tap in time of crisis. Meditation is taken seriously; but this is not prayer. Mental discipline is something we do; it is not a cry for help to some outside power. Reverence and respect for the Buddha are encouraged, but not worship.

Since this is such an important point for an understanding of the Buddha's Path we would do well again to hear the venerable and respected U Thittila put it in his own words:

All through the Buddha's teachings, repeated stress is laid on self-reliance and resolution. Buddhism makes man stand on his own feet, it arouses his self-confidence and energy. The Buddha again and again reminded his followers that there is no one, either in heaven or on earth, who can help them or free them from the result of their past evil deeds. "It is through unshaken perseverance, O Monks, that I have reached the peace supreme. If you also, O Monks, will strive unceasingly, you too will within a short time reach the highest goal of holiness by understanding and realizing it yourselves."

Understanding that neither a god nor ceremonies can help or save him, the true Buddhist finds no place for prayer; he feels compelled to rely on his own effort and thus gains self-confidence. He sees that the tendency to rely on a god or any other imaginary power weakens man's confidence in his own power and lessens his sense of responsibility; he sees that blind faith in any authority leads to stagnation and spiritual lethargy. The Buddhist reaches his goal through perseverance in meditation rather than prayer.[3]

TYPICAL TEXTS FROM THE *DHAMMAPADA*

The best loved book of the Theravada Buddhist tradition is the *Dhammapada*. It holds a place among classical Buddhists similar to that of the *Bhagavad-Gita* among Hindus. The title means, "The Path of Truth *(Dhamma)*." The sayings are believed to be the words of the Lord Buddha. This collection of sayings is to later Buddhist philosophy what the Sermon on the Mount is to subsequent Christian theology. Wherever one dips into this inspirational classic one discovers clear and memorable statements of what we have already found to be a consistent Path.

> 380. Self, indeed, is the protector of self; self, indeed, is one's refuge; control therefore your own self as a merchant, a noble steed.[4]

The image of the self controlling the steed will remind Western readers of Plato's famous description of reason controlling the wild horses of passion.

> 236. Make an island unto yourself; strive quickly;

become wise; purged of stain and passionless, you shall enter the heavenly stage of the Ariyas [the enlightened ones].

238. Make an island unto yourself. Strive without delay; fast; become wise. Purged of stain and passionless, you will not come again to birth and old age.

The contrast between this and John Donne's "No Man is an Island" is dramatic. The emphasis here on self-reliance is a concession to popular speech. At a deeper level, for those more advanced, there is the subtle teaching of *Anatta;* no self, no soul. The persisting sense of some continuing "self" is the last illusion which is eventually stripped off in the freedom of Nirvana.

Those who are making progress in the Path are described in these terms:

406. He who is friendly amongst the hostile, who is peaceful amongst the violent, who is unattached among the attached, him I call a brahmana [enlightened one].

414. He who has passed beyond this quagmire, the ocean of life [*Samsara*], and delusion, who has crossed and gone beyond, who is meditative, free from craving and doubts, who clinging to nought, has attained Nibbana, him I call a brahmana.

Perhaps the epitome of the Buddha's Path is given in this favorite text:

327. Take delight in heedfulness; guard your mind well. Draw yourself out of the evil way like an elephant sunk in the mire.

The water buffalo, straining to pull himself out of a

deep mud-hole, was a familiar sight when I lived in Burma. Sunk deeply in the cool ooze on a blistering hot day, he would in the late afternoon struggle to pull his great body out of the mud. Schoolboys would stand around jeering and throwing sticks and stones. First one great foot would gain a foothold, only to go crashing back into the mud-hole. Many efforts would be of no avail. Finally, after tremendous striving, a proper foothold would be made. The huge body would emerge. He had lifted himself out! The schoolboys' jeers were turned to cheers.

THE BUDDHA'S LAST WORDS

The Buddha died, a gentleman to the end. Tradition has it that he hesitated to eat pork curry in the rainy season, but he refused to be discourteous to his village host. He died at the ripe age of eighty, surrounded by his monks and in great esteem. His last words are held with special honor. Actually they simply reiterate what he had been teaching since his first sermon.

When asked if he had any "hidden wisdom" to give at the very last he said, "I have preached the truth without making any distinction between exoteric and esoteric doctrine. . . . The Tathagatha has no such thing as the closed fist of the teacher who keeps such things back. Why should he lay down instruction in any matter for the Order?"

He then uttered these last words to his followers: "Be ye lamps unto yourselves. Betake yourselves to no external refuge. Hold fast to the truth as a lamp. Hold fast as a refuge to the truth. Look not for refuge to anyone besides yourselves. Behold now, brethren, I exhort you saying: 'Decay is inherent in all component things! Work out your salvation with diligence!' "[5]

NOTES

1. Karl Jaspers, *The Great Philosophers,* Vol. I, *The Foundations,* trans. Ralph Manheim (New York: Harcourt Brace, 1962).

2. Quoted in Kenneth W. Morgan, ed., *The Path of the Buddha* (New York: Ronald, 1956), p. 112.

3. Ibid., pp. 76–77.

4. Quotations from the *Dhammapada* are from the Wisdom of the East edition, trans. Thera Narada (London: John Murray, 1959; New York: Paragon Reprint).

5. From the *Maha-Parinibbana-Sutta,* in the *Digha-Nikaya.* See Henry C. Warren, *Buddhism in Translations* (Cambridge: Harvard University Press, 1953; New York: Atheneum, 1963).

Suggestions for Further Reading

Conze, Edward. *Buddhist Meditations.* Ethical and Religious Classics in East and West. London: Allen and Unwin, 1956; New York: Harper & Row.

The Dhammapada: many translations are available.

King, Winston L. *Buddhism and Christianity: Some Bridges of Understanding.* Philadelphia: Westminster, 1962; Greenwood, S.C.: Attic Press, 1962.

Ross, Nancy. *Three Ways of Asian Wisdom.* New York: Simon and Schuster, 1937, 1966; Millwood, N.Y.: Kraus Reprint.

Smith, Huston, *The Religions of Man.* New York: Harper & Row, 1958.

Walpola, Sri Rahula. *What the Buddha Taught.* Chester Springs, Pa.: Dufour, 1967; rev. ed. New York: Grove, 1974.

4

ZEN: THE PATHLESS PATH
TO AUTHENTIC LIVING

Zen is the Asian Path that has recently had the strongest appeal and influence in the West. It likes to think of itself as "the heart of all religions"; it does not like to be thought of as "just one more religion." In fact, it usually sounds as if it is opposed to "religion," at least formal, established, institutional "religion." It could be described as the "pathless actualization of the authentic." But even this would be much too abstract for Zen people. It would be better to say: "Just ordinary life, only two inches off the ground."

Zen people are quick to warn against wordy professors and writers who try to give historical introductions to Zen. They say this is just the way *not* to understand it! Teachers who describe "it," as if "it" were a doctrine or a religion, only spread confusion; sometimes this confusion is fatal to a beginner. This occupational disease of professors can only spread what they call "The Stink of Zen."

Having paid my respects to this sentiment, let me

48

continue the "Stink" in the hope that some little "click" of understanding might yet come. Zen people, of all people, know that from the most unlikely sources, seemingly by accident, a glimmer of enlightenment might break forth. Even a professor can dare to hope!

Zen Buddhism means *Meditation* Buddhism. In contrast to Theravada Buddhism, which quickly spread to Southeast Asia, Mahayana Buddhism flourished in North India. At that time India was filled with highly developed yoga and meditation methods. One of the sects of the many strands of the Mahayana Buddhist tradition began to especially emphasize *Dyana*, or meditation, as a path to Buddhist enlightenment. This school eventually spread to China, where *Dyana* was called *Ch'an*; later it was carried to Japan, where it was called *Zen*.

THE BUDDHA'S FLOWER SERMON

Zen seeks to "help the lights come on." *Satori* is the word for enlightenment, which is the goal of this tradition; it occupies a place similar to *Nirvana* in the Theravada tradition. But this "seeing" comes in the most uncommon, or even the most common, ways. Sometimes it is a story, a swift kick, a poem, a thunderstorm, a chance conversation—any of a thousand happenings may "trigger" the insight. When it comes it is something like a lock clicking open after a long working of the key.

For this reason I will resort to a number of stories, poems, sayings, and pictures with the hope that, Zen-like, the lock might open, or some light might break.

One day the Lord Buddha was teaching his disciples

on the mountainside. Evidently it was slow going; nothing seemed to be getting through. Then he stopped, picked up a lotus flower, and held it high. All of a sudden one of the monks, named Mahakasyapa, "saw the light."A flash of understanding crossed his face. The Buddha saw that a transmission of light had taken place with a gesture, without words. He recognized in Mahakasyapa his true successor.

Zen people realize that *the deepest cannot be taught, but can be caught.* A similar transmission was carried over to twenty-eight successive patriarchs in India; then carried to China in A.D. 520 by the Indian missionary, Bodhidharma. Eventually this Path spread to Japan in the twelfth century and continues as a living source of insight and power today. In Zen the relationship of teacher to disciple is crucially important. There is a kind of "apostolic succession" of one enlightened person passing on the light to others.

BODHIDHARMA: BUDDHIST MISSIONARY TO CHINA

When Bodhidharma, the twenty-eighth patriarch, traveled to China, several other Buddhist sects were already flourishing. In fact, the Emperor himself was a very zealous propagator of the Buddhist Path.

Being eager to impress the new missionary with his many good works, the Emperor gave Bodhidharma a tour of his buildings. He pointed out the numerous pagodas and monasteries he had built; the number of monks he fed; and the various Scripture translation projects he was sponsoring. Feeling quite proud of his accomplishments he turned to Bodhidharma for a word of approval.

The gruff monk looked out from under his shaggy

eyebrows, glared at the Emperor with the utmost contempt and snorted: "Rubbish! You haven't really done anything!"

Following this, tradition says, he retired to Mt. Su and meditated for the next nine years with his face to the wall!

Zen has no confidence in sweaty self-righteousness! Zeal for the externals of religion, it feels, is usually a way of separating oneself from the real and the authentic. Religious busybodies are a plague!

Emperors, and those trapped by establishment roles are, of all people, the most to be pitied. They cannot really be *themselves*; they must play the roles assigned to them, wear the clothes, and say the words that society demands of them. They are not free. Perhaps they can be shaken loose; shocked into seeing their bondage for what it is.

Meditation is a skill to be cultivated. Beyond books, debates, and ritual, the quiet waiting enables the realization of who one is; it allows the light to break forth.

TAOISM PAVES THE WAY FOR ZEN'S PATHLESS PATH

There was good reason why Zen caught hold in China and soon became one of the leading Buddhist schools. The Chinese are frequently described as a people with two pulse-beats: the Confucian and the Taoist. Lin Yutang has said of his people: "The Confucianist in us builds and strives; while the Taoist in us watches and smiles. When a scholar is in his office he moralizes, when he comes home from his office he writes poetry, and it is usually good Taoist poetry."[1]

Confucianism encouraged the art of good form in personal and social relationships. The quality of life was the result of learning the graces of appropriate behavior. The Chinese are masters of the art of personal relations. But deep-down the Chinese were much more than models of correct etiquette. The other half of them longed for harmony with nature, the free-flowing quality of the streams, and the expansive lightness of the rising mists on the mountain tops. The Taoist half reached out for quietness, simplicity, freedom, and spontaneity.

Lao Tzu, "The Old Boy," was spokesman for this side of the Chinese nature. The beautiful collection of eighty poems attributed to him, the *Tao Teh Ching*, is, next to the Christian Bible, the most frequently translated book in the world. Its beauty and suggestive power have spoken to every generation since it first appeared. It is now more widely read in the West than in any previous period. This small collection of poems is the finest place to "catch" the deepest current of Chinese wisdom.

The flowing stream is a key metaphor for Taoism. One is to "flow with" the *Tao*, or life-principle of the universe. To be "with it," not "against the *Tao*," is to be fulfilled. Not rigidity and aggressiveness, but flexibility and simple naturalness are encouraged. To "get ahead" it is best to lie low and keep quiet.

The curse of life is the many layers of artificiality of which cities are the symbol: the impersonal relationships; the dictated tastes of custom; the abstractions of bureaucracy and technological civilization. Wisdom resides with the simple, uncomplicated people who are close to the soil and who move with the rhythms of nature; not the wordy professors, the politically ambitious "climbers," and the scheming, overweight moneylenders. To live in harmony with the *Tao*—the really real—is the path to authenticity.

To a people constitutionally half-Taoist the emphases of Zen seemed very natural and congenial. Another way of putting it would be to say that, while Buddhism generally was a "foreign religion" which came from India to China, by the time the Chinese took it over and gave it their own imprint it became, especially in Meditation (*Ch'an*) Buddhism, a very natural, Chinese path to the authentic.

HUI NENG: ZEN IN CHINESE GARMENT

Hui Neng was a poor boy, without a father, who lived in southern China about A.D. 700. He supported his mother by selling wood. One day he discovered some lines from the famous Buddhist Scripture, the Diamond Sutra, which stirred a keen interest in the deepest questions of life. He determined to travel to a famous Buddhist monastery in the north, where he could learn more of the wisdom of this Path.

He was met at the gate by the exceedingly gruff Abbot who, noticing his southern accent, said: "So you are a southerner! Don't you know that *no* southerners have the Buddha nature! How can *you* expect to be a Buddha?"

Tradition says that the poor orphan looked the famous Abbot squarely in the face and said: "There may be southerners and northerners; but as far as the Buddha nature goes there is no difference!"

The Abbot pondered this unintimidated boy and said in effect: "Well, we can use you here. Yes, indeed!

We have a place in the monastery for your type. Get back to the kitchen and pound rice and clean up the pots and pans!"

Hui Neng did this for some time. Eventually there came a competition to see who had the keenest insight into Zen matters. The one whose poem revealed the deepest understanding would become Abbot of the monastery and the new Sixth Patriarch of China. In spite of severe jealousy among the monks, Hui Neng was the abbot's first choice. So, in time, he came to be one of the foremost Zen masters.

With Hui Neng, Zen became much more thoroughly Chinese. Meditation Buddhism took on Chinese garment. The basic formula was summed up in these words:

> "No dependence upon the words and letters;
> A special transmission outside the classified teachings;
> Direct pointing to the mind of man;
> Seeing into one's own nature."

To "see into one's own nature" was to realize that the Buddha nature was all-pervasive, like the *Tao* or the *Brahmin*. It pervades the world and so it pervades all people. We are potentially *Tao*, or authentically real, or "Buddha." Since we *are* that, we must allow that *to be*. The "direct pointing of the mind" is to allow the real to emerge from the encrustations of the phony and artificial which cloud the brightness of the original mirror.

Hui Neng and his followers stress the fact that insight or *Satori* comes abruptly. This seeing or "falling into place" cannot be conjured up or routinely programed into an educational curriculum. He said: "We talk of seeing into our own nature, not of practicing meditation or obtaining liberation; not *Dyana* or *Nirvana*." Abrupt awakening came to characterize what was called the "Southern School" of Hui Neng.

In contrast, the "Northern School" came to emphasize the carefully cultivated methods of meditation. Rigorous discipline was encouraged. This was the school which in time came to strongly influence Japanese culture. To this day in Japan these differences characterize the "Gradual School" (Soto Zen) and the "Abrupt School" (Rinzai Zen).

THE SIMPLIFICATION OF LIFE

A perfect Zen-story would be the Old Testament account of David and his sling-shot. When the hearty young shepherd boy appeared at the battle scene he encountered the established methods of warfare. Before his brothers (supposedly older and wiser) would allow him to fight the giant, Goliath, they covered him with layers and loads of their cumbersome armor. This was the *only* way to do battle with such an overpowering foe! But David soon realized that he could not move freely or "do his own thing" if he was dominated by others' styles. So he wisely shed the armor that had been forced on him. Then, armed only with his sling-shot, he moved with confidence to face the giant. In short order he had done, in his own way, what the conventional of his day could never accomplish.

Zen people believe we are everywhere in and penetrated by the Buddha-nature (the *Tao*, the *Dharma*, or, if one prefers, the Creative Spirit or the Kingdom of God). This is what really *is*, and this is what we really *are*. But this authentic life gets buried, stifled, warped, and smothered by the overlays of artificiality which society early begins to heap on us.

As one moves up the scale of social responsibility and prominence these artificialities increase. This is why for Zen people the symbols of the authentic life are the child, the peasant, and the tramp. The least likely to be "real" are the bishop, the dean, the company president, and the "top politicians."

Formal education, especially as prescribed by "schools," and particularly those which are acutely aware of the official accrediting agencies, is exactly the path that thwarts originality and spontaneity. Jesus (who appears very much the Zen-man) observed that it was almost impossible for a rich man to enter the Kingdom. For the same reason it is nearly impossible, Zen people would say, to survive a graduate school program for a Ph.D. degree without being maimed for life by an inner warping.

Zen calls for a stripping down: a losing of excess weight; a taking of a critical look at current success-symbols; a lessening of concern to look over the shoulder to see if others are granting approval. Nothing need be done to coax the Buddha nature. Light is everywhere seeking to break through into *Satori* when the slightest opening is given. But the negative "clearing of the way," or simplification of life, is a positive step in the direction of the Path.

This attitude explains the constant "jabbing" and balloon-pricking that fills Zen poetry. Shock-treatment is necessary to pierce the heavy armor of respectability that encases us in our straightjackets. With wry humor Zen poets seek to puncture windbags with the hope of opening one to the authentic. Reminders of our common humanity are salutary experiences; they deflate the pretensions by which we fool ourselves, while fooling nobody else.

The Japanese Haiku Poet Buson wrote:

> The Archbishop
>> Evacuates his honorable bowels
>>> On the withered moor.

Again,

> "I am the first cicada,"
>> He said,
>>> And piddled!

SITTING QUIETLY, DOING NOTHING

Meditation enables one to gear-down to the rhythms of nature; it permits an open responsiveness to the call of the real. In a way this is "doing nothing." In other ways it is choosing the path which alone leads to the increasingly significant and authentic.

> Sitting quietly, doing nothing
>> Spring comes and the grass grows by itself.

Nature produces in its own way, in its own time, and with incredible diversity.

> In the Landscape of spring
>> The flowering branches grow naturally,
>>> Some long, some short.

Living in this way reduces competition with others or concern to be measured by the norms of a diseased society. Rather, it increases sensitivity to the union of the outer and inner natures.

> In Spring the flowers, in Autumn the moon.
>> In Summer refreshing breeze, in Winter snow.
>> What else do I have need of?
>> Each hour to me is an hour of joy.

UNFRANTIC ENERGY:
THE FLOWING, SPONTANEOUS LIFE

Zen people do not prescribe a set of rules or a pre-packaged style of life. We are not to clutter our lives with religious "extras."

> How wondrously supernatural and how miraculous this is;
>> I draw water, I carry fuel.
>
> When you finish eating, wash your bowl.

Religious exercises often add to the load of unreality which clings like barnacles to an old ship. Even otherwise good things like "Scriptures" can be used to substitute someone else's jargon for honest thought and authentic expression. Some people desperately need "saving" from meditation-schedules and Scripture-quoting. (There may be others who could profit from learning a judicious use of these, and other methods!)

The Master Hsuan-Chen wrote with typical Zen-abruptness:

> When thirsty—drink; when hungry—eat; when the time comes—pass water; when tired—go to sleep. Nirvana and Bodhi are just dead stumps to which you can tie your jackass. The paper of Scripture is put to best use when used for wiping pus from boils.

One of the favorite Zen paintings is of the monk with great zest and glee ripping to bits the pages of the

Scriptures. To dismiss this as irreverence would be to miss the main point. It is the Zen response to the mood which informs the Christian hymn: "Beyond the sacred page, I seek thee, Lord."

This appreciation for the ordinary rather than the "extras" is closely related to what Christians have called "the sacramental quality of *all* life." Perhaps the most Zen-like man in the Christian tradition was the simple Brother Lawrence, the sixteenth-century Carmelite who, like Hui Neng in China, did kitchen chores in the monastery kitchen. He discovered, and soon those about him also discovered, that the time of prayer was not different from the time of work, but in the noise and clutter of his kitchen he could be as close to God as on his knees before the Blessed Sacrament.

The effect of this is to greatly reduce the strain and stress of life and allow one to be more *really present* in all that is done. Instead of frantic activity where "one's heart is not in it," one is *really present* in what is going on. This has the effect of seeming to slow one down; actually it gives time and space for a free "flow with" the situation, which means a larger degree of spontaneity. One runs less, but goes further. Another way of putting it would be to say there is less busyness on the surface, and more responsiveness in the depths.

> If a man in the morning embrace the *Tao*,
> Then he may die in the evening without regret.

A PICTURE IS WORTH A THOUSAND WORDS

The Chinese are masters of the art of personal relations and the world's most prolific poets. They also know the value of pictures to communicate meaning.

One of the best ways to sense the Zen spirit is to look responsively at one of the Zen-Taoist nature paintings which embody this Path.

Looking at the creation made with a few simple brush strokes we see the mountains rising, tier after tier, up and away into the misty heights. A forest glen with a running stream is seen in the lower right. We quickly sense an "aliveness" in the quiet composure of the painting. There is a rhythmic vitality which is the fusion of the rhythm of the *Tao* with the movement of living things. We are caught up in this life as we respond to its rhythms.

Laurence Binyon, in commenting on this kind of painting, has written:

> In these paintings we do not feel that the artist is portraying something external to himself; that he is caressing the happiness and soothing joy offered him in the pleasant places of earth, or even studying with wonder and delight the miraculous works of nature. But the winds of the air have become his desires, and the clouds his wandering thoughts; the mountain-peaks are his lonely aspirations, and the torrents his liberated energies. Flowers, opening their secret hearts to the light and trembling to the breeze's touch, seem to be unfolding the mystery of his own human heart, the mystery of those intuitions and emotions which are too deep or too shy for speech. It is not one aspect or another of nature, one particular beauty or another: the pleasant sward and leafy glade are not chosen and the austere crags and caves, with the wild beasts that haunt them, left and avoided. It is not men's earthly surroundings, tamed to his desires, that inspire the artist; but the universe, in its wholeness and its freedom, has become his spiritual home.[2]

It would be easy to see it all and miss the slight human figure, ever so small in the total scheme of things. But he is there; not dominating in any sense, but integral to the whole scene. Perhaps he is a sage sitting quietly by the lotus pond, or the farmer crossing the rickety bridge or ascending the slope. There is a harmony—not a jarring contrast—between the inner and the outer, the natural and the human, as all, in diverse ways, express the *Tao*, or Buddha-nature. All that is strained and strident has been eased. Emptiness is identical with fullness. The silence, say of the winter snow, speaks the same word. The path disappears in the distance, because even the persistence of the Path is not the most important thing. The Path is at best a "finger pointing to the moon."

NOTES

1. Lin Yutang, *My Country and My People* (New York: John Day, 1935), p. 55.
2. Laurence Binyon, *The Flight of the Dragon: An Essay on the Theory and Practice of Art in China and Japan*, Wisdom of the East Series (New York: Grove, 1961), pp. 24-25.

Suggestions for Further Reading

Herrigel, Eugene. *The Method of Zen.* Edited by R. F. Hull and Alan Watts. New York: Random House, 1974.

5

THE CHRISTIAN WAY:
UNIQUE AND UNIVERSAL

This chapter is bound to be different from the last three. I now write as an "insider" rather than an "outsider." In some ways this chapter is much easier for me to write; in other ways it is much more difficult. I think it will be best if I begin by sharing something of my struggle in writing it. (This is my third attempt! I am now in Hong Kong in my new assignment!) By sharing my own struggle it may help the reader to be more sympathetic with what I have attempted to do. It will also encourage readers to criticize my effort, which is one of the best forms of education. Since my basic aim is to encourage fresh thought, I believe this aim can be best furthered by a frank sharing of myself.

I am a missionary at heart. I was named by my parents after the missionary apostle, Paul. I am sure that the heritage of the home of a missionary-minded Baptist pastor has colored all of my subsequent interests and decisions. My first interests in Asia, especially China, were kindled by hearing my mother read missionary letters and articles in magazines concerned with Christian missionaries in Asia. I was, of course, quite free to ignore or reject these concerns. But in time I came to accept them, sift and reformulate them, but basically make them my own.

Sometimes it seems a long road from those days in a small-town parsonage in Michigan to my present position of teaching *both* Christian Theology *and* the History of Asian Religions in the Chinese University of Hong Kong. But for all the distance and differences, I see continuities all the way. My life as a missionary and a professor has been fairly equally divided between East and West. My teaching experience has also been fairly equally divided between interpreting the Christian faith as a theologian, and seeking to interpret the Asian Paths as fairly as possible in both East and West. Wherever I have lived and worked I have discovered the need for *both* of these tasks. It has fallen to my lot to try to do both and to seek to keep these tasks closely related. Although at times I feel thoroughly stretched, I have sensed that the integration of these concerns is an important part of a missionary vocation. This is what I live with; this is who I am.

In the past three chapters I have tried to interpret, as fairly and sympathetically as possible, three of the time-honored, growing, renewed Asian Paths. Now I must try to do some kind of justice to the Christian Way in which I seek to live as a committed believer and a missionary. I am somewhat fearful that while I have made the other faiths seem "interesting" this presentation may be dull by comparison. This might be due to my lack of power as a Christian interpreter. It might also happen because of the reader's long familiarity with some version of the Christian faith. So often our past experience, especially bad experiences, blurs our vision and dulls our capacity to really understand the Christian faith afresh.

There is another peril of which I am very conscious. To describe the Christian Way in one brief chapter means I must select a few themes out of many possibilities. This will reveal my own special interests, limitations, and biases. Some readers may say, "He didn't even mention . . ." and then add their favorite theme.

But having shared something of my problems and hesitations, I am pressing on boldly. My aim is twofold: to heed the sigh of my namesake, "Woe to me if I do not preach the Gospel!" (1 Cor. 9:16); and to pray the prayer of my favorite saint, Francis of Assisi, "Help me not so much to seek to be understood, as to understand."

In selecting a few basic themes of the Christian Way my aim is to stress the most foundational elements of what C. S. Lewis has taught us to call "Mere Christianity." I am most interested in what is central to the main, historic, tradition of all Christians; not what is the peculiar emphasis of certain sects, or some recent fad. I identify completely with C. S Lewis in his preface to *Mere Christianity* when he wrote: "For I was not writing to expound something I could call 'my religion,' but to expound 'mere' Christianity, which is what it is and what it was long before I was born and whether I like it or not."[1]

I want to try to be true to the central missionary tradition of the Christian community and do justice to both the *uniqueness* and the *universality* of the Christian faith. To try to do a measure of justice to *both* of these concerns constitutes the perennial lure and permanent frustration of the missionary vocation. (I know in advance that my aim will vastly outreach my achievement!) The Christian Gospel is *different* from other perspectives and paths. But in the deepest sense it *fulfills* whatever God-given quests and insights are embodied in these other paths. The Way is meant for all and is capable of being a "home" for all. The Way is not a time-bound, culture-bound, exclusive religious sect. It is both unique and universal; and these are meant to be kept together. To try to fairly interpret this is a tall order! I want to make the effort.

THE COMMUNITY OF THE RESURRECTION

The Community of Worship and Work

From the first day of the movement Christians were known as followers of "the Way" (Acts 9:2; 19:9, 23; 22:4; 24:14, 22). The Way meant a distinctive style of life. It included a new viewpoint, new values, fresh zest for living and, above all, new ways of relating to people. The Way meant a life together; it was inescapably communal. All members of the Way had a special relationship to a Person—Jesus of Nazareth, who had been crucified, but who was believed, by members of the community, to be a living, powerful presence. His presence or his Spirit animated the new community. He was close to each individual as a most caring and helpful friend or counselor.

Sometimes Jesus Christ was spoken of as "the Way." The Gospel of John has him saying: "I am the way, and the truth, and the life" (John 14:6).[2] During Jesus' days as a wandering teacher in Palestine he had a very mixed assortment of disciples. Some were fishermen and tax collectors; others were revolutionaries, who hoped for the overthrow of the Roman political establishment. In his lifetime these only partially understood his teachings; frequently they badly misunderstood him. But after his death on the cross as a criminal and the Easter Day of the Resurrection the understanding of these disciples was greatly transformed. They now saw more clearly and more deeply than they could possibly have seen when they walked with him physically on the shores of the Lake of Galilee or the streets of Jerusalem. In time others came to see and believe as they did. These others also found themselves in relationship to this living Lord. The new community was quickly enlarged.

Easter Day made all the difference in the world! (This statement is true on many levels.) Before it had been Jesus of Nazareth and his confused followers. Now it became the living Lord, powerfully present through his Spirit, in the new community. This community could be rightly called "the Community of the Resurrection," or "the Lord's people," or those of "the Way." This community continues to live today.

As Christians the center of our life is the living Lord and the Easter faith. People of other Paths often make visits to temples and pilgrimages to sacred places. Special rituals are set aside for morning, evening, and festival days. We are surrounded by all kinds of religious observances. But the Community of the Resurrection has its own special style. Each week members of the Way meet to celebrate the Easter event. Ever since the first Easter morning Christians have continued to meet, without a break in continuity, on what we call "The Lord's Day." We remember his triumph over death, evil, and darkness; we hear the Good News (the Gospel) afresh. We celebrate the re-creating power of God by song and prayers of thanksgiving. Each week since Easter Day some Christians have helped to keep the Easter Faith alive by re-doing "The Lord's Supper." By means of this simple community meal of bread and wine we re-present (make present again) the living Lord with his followers. There is an unbroken testimony, since the first Easter Day, that he is not only remembered as a past figure of history but is somehow, mysteriously but really, *present* in his community now as a life-giving power in the simple act of "the breaking of bread." This "Lord's Supper" came to be called "The Eucharist," which is the Greek word for "thanksgiving." Our central act of worship is a thanksgiving for what the Lord and Life-giver (as the Nicene Creed puts it) *has done* and *is continually doing.*

We do not think of ourselves as a religious cult following the teachings of a first-century peasant preacher in Palestine. We believe that in those events, centering in the cross and the resurrection of our Lord, God, or the Creative Power of the Universe, was acting in a unique way to renew the world. So we join with the Community of the Resurrection throughout the world and sing: "Glory be to the Father, and to the Son, and to the Holy Spirit; as it was in the beginning, is now, and ever shall be, world without end. Amen." The living Lord is the clue, or window, through which we see and reunite with the ever renewing Creative Spirit.

The Community of the Resurrection returns from its worship to its work in the world. We see all of our work to be, in some sense, "the Lord's service." Most of us do ordinary tasks; we are teachers, farmers, office workers, factory workers, artists, mechanics—in short, butchers and bakers and candlestick-makers. But in our places we seek and hope to be "instruments" through which the Creative Spirit continues to work.

We know that the Way has made us one with each other and one in the Lord's service. From the earliest days of the movement the figure of "the one body" has been used to describe our relationship to each other and to our Lord. We are members (with a wide variety of gifts and functions) of the "Body of Christ." He is the head; we are the various members. We are to be instruments to carry out the purposes of the head. Far from finding the Lord's service to be a great burden, this turns out to be the most fulfilling life. To be an "ambassador for Christ" (2 Cor. 5:20) and a "fellow worker for God" (1 Cor. 3:9) is life's highest calling. His service turns out to be perfect freedom! Less than this is to be less than fully alive!

The Language of the Community

The Community of the Resurrection has freely used all kinds of word-pictures to explain and communicate its message. We are not compelled to keep using the earliest words or symbols; we are urged to speak the language of our day and fashion new metaphors. But each generation has a way of finding fresh meaning in some of the oldest figures of speech. Our use of language, then, is more poetic, suggestive, and liturgical than it is exact and scientific. In poetry and in faith-expressions we take words and symbols seriously, but not always literally. Sometimes the literal would kill the meaning, while the poetic use would keep it alive and fresh for generations to come. We use words to hint at what could never be adequately "pinned down" in a definition.

Take, for instance, the earliest creed of the community: "Jesus Christ is Lord" (Rom. 10:9; 1 Cor. 12:3; Phil. 2:11). For Jewish-background people "Lord" had the sense of God, Creator, divine. For the growing number of Roman-background people "Lord" was the same word as was used for the Emperor, Caesar. So this simple creed had immense political implications. If Jesus was Lord, then Caesar was not the final authority. He was a human leader who might well need to be criticized or opposed. Early Christians were often accused of being potentially rebellious because they affirmed that Jesus Christ, not Caesar, was "Lord" (Acts 17:7).

Today we still use these words. This is the official creedal basis for the World Council of Churches. In our personal lives we speak of Jesus Christ as Lord, meaning we belong wholly to Jesus Christ and seek always to be servants of the creative purposes of God.

Another early, powerful Greek word used by the community was "*Logos.*" Jesus Christ is the *Logos.* This is hard to translate. It has sometimes been translated as "the Word of God." It could also be described as the creative, ordering principle of the universe. This all-embracing word is similar to the *Dharma* of India or the *Tao* of China. When we use this we would be saying that Jesus Christ is the inner power or creative energy of the universe.

Sometimes this idea was put more simply: Jesus Christ is the "visible image of the invisible God" (Col. 1:15). By this we mean, when we see Jesus we see, as it were, the face of God. Jesus becomes the window to see into the heart of God, or the pulsating center of the universe (John 1:15, 18; 14:9; 2 Cor. 4:6).

The Gospel of John is in many ways the simplest, but also the most profound, of the early writings that continue to nourish our hearts and imaginations. The expressions in this book are the most universal or common. Jesus Christ is described as the *Light.* He is the light of the world and this light shines within our hearts; this light will never be blacked-out (John 1:1–9; 8:12). He is the *Life* of the world. He is the source, sustainer, and re-creative energy of all that is good. He is *Love.* His caring is the source of all good. He comes first and steadily to free the enslaved, forgive the guilty, and draw us out of the prison of self-love into the care and concern for others. Since he is all of these he is also the *Power.* The Greek word was *dynamis,* from which our word "dynamite" comes. He is the concentrated energy, the explosive force which breaks-up, in order to make new.

Now what is especially significant to understand is that these metaphors are strikingly similar to the most basic ones used in describing the Asian Paths. The word "Buddha," as we have seen, means to be *enlightened.* To develop the Buddha-nature means to live and walk as an enlightened one. The Hindus speak of Vishnu as *love,* who in saving mercy becomes incarnate in many forms. Zen seeks to encourage authentic *life.* All seek contact or relationship with the source of all *life,* called the *Dharma* or the *Tao* of the universe. This is the *power* that enables life to develop, grow, and mature.

Interestingly, when we use the oldest, richest word-pictures to describe the *uniqueness* of the Way, we are using the most cherished and most *universal* terms of the Asian Paths. To be sure, new content has been poured into the old vessels. But our very words seem to imply that when we understand the *uniqueness* of the Way we are also closest to its most *universal* understanding.

The Central Symbols of the Community

The Community of the Resurrection has two central symbols: the cross and the resurrection. The deepest experience of life is to pass through a death to old ways and be reborn to new ways. The power of the community, and the power of our personal lives, arises from a fresh understanding and application of the dying-rising life.

When the Life-giving Spirit was incarnated as Jesus of Nazareth he was despised and rejected as a fanatic and a political revolutionary. He was crucified in the manner of a common criminal (the cross) by a combination of the Jewish religious establishment and the Roman political establishment. The cross was the way of death.

Taken by itself the cross of Jesus might be taken as a symbol of tragedy. It points to the fact that in a cruel and brutal world the most innocent of people often suffer at the hands of people who are loaded with good intentions for religious orthodoxy and political security.

But Easter Day caused everything to be seen in a new light. It meant that the tragedy of the cross was not the last word. Even the Friday of the cross could, from the new perspective, be seen as Good Friday. Beyond the most tragic there was the possibility of new beginnings.

The power of God, or the universe, is on the side of bringing new life out of old. Self-giving may involve the utmost of suffering; but in this way, perhaps only in this way, new life can be brought to birth.

Dying, then, is the costly path to rebirth. It is through Jesus Christ that we have learned most clearly about the dying-rising life. In contact with him, as members of the Community of the Resurrection, we grow in understanding of this life and we are made into channels of this recreative power in the world.

As we look about we find that the symbol of the cross seems to predominate in the art and architecture of the world. Churches and cathedrals are often built in the shape of the cross. We place the cross on the top of church buildings. People wear necklaces or pins using the symbol of the cross. Some Christians learn to use a nonverbal means of expression: the sign of the cross. All of this is understandable. We can believe it and begin to experience it in our lives; but it can never be proved nor adequately described or explained. No art or verbal formula can do it justice. Still, the two belong together. The cross can only be properly understood as part of the death-rebirth rhythm.

If we live in the light and power of these central symbols our whole way of life will be radically re-shaped. This may not happen all at once; we are slow learners at best. We will do everything we possibly can to defend what we now are, so as to avoid the costly experience of change and rebirth. But when the change comes it is radical. "Radical" is an accurate word. It means going to the root, or center. For us to begin and increasingly live the dying-rising life is to draw upon the power of the center-point, the heart of life, the source of re-creating vitality. This is to live by the power of "Our Lord the Spirit" (Charles Williams' fine phrase for it).

The Asian Paths have also had a vivid sense that it is always the "Middle Way" which leads to enlightenment and deliverance. To be "hung up" or trapped by the extremes is to be cut off from the real flow of life where the action is. For instance, to close our eyes to evil, sin, and suffering would lead to a false optimism. Our vision would be distorted by our unwillingness to see deeply. This would be a life of illusion. But a dark pessimism about the possibilities of change and rebirth would be equally futile. Cynical pessimism is deadly. The Community of the Resurrection moves in the radical middle between the traps of illusion and hopelessness. This creative middle is a realistic view which knows both the cross and the resurrection. Life drawn from this center has the freshness of the new and is pervaded by Easter joy.

We will need to experience this death to the old and rebirth of the new again and again. It will not happen once-for-all. It is not easy to pass from adolescence to maturity. It is easy to acquiesce in a kind of permanent adolescence. Mature, adult, responsible life is not easy to bear. But through death to one stage, we enter another stage. In being parents to our children we are tempted to act as if we are all-wise, to play God. But we will surely have to pass through the difficult experience of dying to much of our old wisdom. We will have to face the inadequacy of our own achievements. We may even have to face and learn from our own failures, instead of defensively explaining them as due to the faults of others. It may shake us up to discover our children to be our best teachers. But this could be a means of rebirth for us. We will be called upon to pass through changes in social and political life. We will perhaps cling fearfully to the old. But it may be necessary to die and be born again if we are to be parts of a new future, not simply relics, or museum-pieces, of a dying period. Eventually we will have to face the fact of our physical death. This can be frightening. But if, along the way, we have discovered that it is through death that we come to new forms of life, we will be able to face physical death also with a serene and quiet courage.

The cross and the resurrection are symbols of the deepest in life. Learning this is our most difficult lesson. But from this springs our deepest joy, confidence, and hope.

The Community: Royal Priesthood, Holy Nation

The Community of the Resurrection lives as a distinct and unique society *in the midst* of the vast network of interlocking social groups of our world. The community has its own ethos, history, evolving language, life style (or styles), heroes, and practices. To be a member of this community does not, by any means, call for a retreat from society. It calls for a special way of *being in* society.

The purpose of the community is to live-out, or body-forth, the Good News of the re-creating goodness and power of God, which we have seen focused in the life-death-resurrection of Jesus Christ. The community is a human medium, or instrument, of a divine communication. To live in this community means to draw life from the creative center of life. This is to live "where the action is." There is no chance to escape in isolation to the fringes of society.

One of the early Christian writings described the purpose of the Way in these bold and suggestive figures. "But you are a chosen race, a royal priesthood, a holy nation, God's own people, that you may declare the wonderful deeds of him who called you out of darkness into his marvellous light" (1 Peter 2:9). The Book of Revelation includes a hymn sung in praise of Jesus Christ saying:

> ". . . . for thou wast slain and by thy blood didst ransom men for God
> from every tribe and tongue and people and nation,
> and hast made them a kingdom and priests to our God,
> and they shall reign on earth" (Rev. 5:9, 10).

The Community of the Resurrection is called to be a nation, or a people, *among the peoples.* It is a people with a special function—to be a priestly people.

A priest is a representative person. He is not necessarily better or even different. But through certain choices and decisions he is set aside to perform special functions. He represents all the people and he performs a mediating function. He represents and voices the needs, anxieties, sins, and aspirations *of the people* before the altar. Then he represents (re-presents, makes-present-again) *to the people* the wisdom, power, and mercy which surround them and are at work in their lives.

This figure of the priestly people gives a striking clue to the purpose of the Community of the Resurrection. This community is drawn from the people; it shares the whole range of human problems and struggles. But its function is to be a representative people. It lives with a heightened awareness of human struggles, sins, and hopes. But it exists to mediate the Good News; "to declare the wonderful deeds" of the Re-creating One who seeks to call all out of darkness into light.

In its representative capacity the community performs, in a sense *for* all people, what all *should* do, and in their most sensitive moments perceive as good. All *should* worship with reverence and gratitude the mysterious source of life. This community *does* this daily, whether others are aware of it or not. All *should* listen to the continuous communication which the Lord of Life is speaking. This community *has as its task* the fresh listening and interpreting of the living Word of God. All *should* live thankfully and obediently a life of useful service. This community *seeks to be* a "Eucharistic" (thankful) and serving body in the thick of the world's needs and struggles.

This is the high and homely calling of the priestly people! But, alas, we who seek to be a part of it know all too well how frequently we become "disobedient to the heavenly vision" (Acts 26:19). In our carelessness and sloth we may become like salt which has lost its flavor (Matt. 5:13). We cease to perform our representative, priestly function. The perennial temptation of the community is to retreat from this demanding center of life and head for the seeming safety and security of the suburbs and fringes of the world. When this happens the community tends to be just another of the numerous, odd religious groups which spawn all over the world. It has then lost its uniqueness and distinction and settled for a place as one religion among many others. Instead of being in the midst of the peoples, it becomes walled-off like a selective religious club—separated by its creeds, customs, and social classes—sometimes interesting, often odd, usually exclusive, eventually boring.

When this happens the only hope for the community is the hope of renewal and resurrection! But, happily, this is always the chief business of Our Lord the Spirit! Then the community must again experience the death of its old life of distortion; and rise again to a fresh understanding of its mediating task. It must listen again, in repentance and faith (openness), to the Good News. After it has reappropriated the Gospel, it will share the Good News again with genuine conviction. The Community of the Resurrection itself lives the dying-rising life. It is healthy when it is undergoing "continuous reformation."

The Community of the Resurrection is a ray of hope, a healthy cell, a creative ferment in the midst of the inevitable drift toward sluggishness and stagnation. One of the earliest symbols of the Way was the fish. The movement (and when it is alive it is "a movement") has the quality of a live fish swimming against the strong current. Its spirit is that of the prayer of one of our most hearty and joyful representatives, St. Francis of Assisi: Lord, make us instruments of Thy peace:

> where there is hatred, let us sow love;
> where there is injury, pardon;
> where there is doubt, faith;
> where there is darkness, light;
> where there is despair, hope;
> where there is sadness, joy.

O Divine Master, grant that we may not so much seek
to be comforted as to comfort; to be understood, as to
understand; to be loved, as to love. For it is in giving
that we receive; it is in pardoning that we are par-
doned; it is in dying that we are born again to eternal
life.

THE DRAMA OF THE DIVINE-HUMAN ENCOUNTER

As followers of the Way we believe we have been
given the clue to the deepest realities of life. We believe
a revealing light has been thrown on the most profound forces in our own lives personally and upon
history generally. From the perspective of the Way we
learn to see life as always moving and always dramatic.
Significant happenings are taking place and we are
actors, not spectators, in the unfolding drama. Our
responses become important parts of the on-going
story.

A great story is being unfolded. The theme of the
story is that the Creative Spirit—God—is now acting to
re-create and renew the world. As this story comes to
us we discover that we are involved as actors, not
watching from the safe distance of the spectators' seats.
All around us, and in us, are evidences of disorder,
disease, disintegration, and disruption. "Dis–" describes a break from the intention or possibilities which
should be realized. But the ever-creating Lord of Life
is continuously caring and coming into the situation to
re-create, revive life, restore order, reintegrate what is
meant to be united, redeem—in short, to bring resurrection. "Re–" shows the possibility of finding again
the original intention and realizing new possibilities.

The living, moving quality of life is the result of the

tireless, unfrantic energy of the Lord of Life. He lives and moves and "in him we live and move and have our being" (Acts 17:28). The dramatic quality of life is seen in the fact that we must respond to what is happening and become actors. Our responses are free, unforced and unprogramed. Our decisions will determine the quality of our lives and affect the stories of other people.

Life means significant encounters. The deepest encounter is *The Divine-Human Encounter*. (This phrase comes from the English title of a famous book by a Swiss theologian, Emil Brunner.) Our response to this encounter will affect every aspect of our lives. The Gospel of John describes this dramatic encounter with the utmost simplicity. "The true light that enlightens every man was coming into the world. He was in the world, and the world was made through him, yet the world knew him not. He came to his own home, and his own people received him not. But to all who received him, who believed in his name, he gave power to become children of God; who were born, not of blood, nor of the will of the flesh, nor of the will of man, but of God" (John 1:9–13).

The great story originates in the ceaseless *caring* of the light and love which is the creative center of the universe. The drama unfolds in the receiving or resisting of this light and love. This is the oldest and deepest story: the Divine-Human Encounter. Followers of the Way believe that this old story is seen in sharpest focus in the coming of God through Jesus Christ into the world, and in the story that unfolds from this central event. This story is continuous; the drama is being enacted today.

No still-picture can do justice to this moving drama in which we are involved. It takes a moving-picture. One of the most vivid pictures of this encounter is found in the last book of the New Testament, the Book of Revelation. "Behold, I stand at the door and knock; if any one hears my voice and opens the door, I will come in to him and eat with him, and he with me" (Rev. 3:20).

The first frame of the moving picture shows the Creative Spirit—Our Lord the Spirit—caring and taking the initiative to come to us. Just why the life-giver should be intrinsically caring, healing, and compassionate is a mystery forever beyond our comprehension. But we have learned that this is so. Creative compassion comes and knocks. But it is always courteous; it never forces its way in.

The second frame shows the human hearing and responding. To be human and in relationship to God means to have response-ability. We can and must respond. We have the power to determine the kind of response. We eventually decide whether we will live an open-door existence or a closed-door existence. Divine compassion and human freedom are the two great mysteries and wonders of life. For God to create oceans, mountains, and roses is one thing; to create people with genuine responsibility involves something else!

The third frame shows the effect of saying yes to the gracious knock. The picture is that of the most universal act—eating a meal together. The shared meal depicts the shared life of fellowship and communion.

The Way sees with uncanny clarity this rhythm or drama of Love's enconter. In the language of the Way, *faith* means saying yes to Love's coming. This means an open-door existence characterized by communion and sharing. *Unbelief* means saying no to life. This means a closed-door existence which makes fellowship and communion impossible.

What we soon discover is that our life is filled with numerous encounters, all of which give us the opportunity to grow and unfold, or to close ourselves and shrivel. The two ways, the way of life and the way of death, encounter us in all kinds of daily situations—in our family experiences, our friendships, our work, our jobs, our temptations, our discouragements. God comes to us in re-creating power in and through real life encounters. We are constantly making decisions for either the open-door or closed-door life.

Significantly, what the Way has seen so clearly of this rhythm and drama has also been known, at least partially, in the various Asian Paths. The Hindu Path has the vivid sense of Vishnu's (Love's) coming, first and always, to help needy humanity. Tagore's "He comes, comes, ever comes," could well be used as an Advent and Christmas shout of praise. The Theravada Buddhist Path has stressed the necessity to live by responsible, free choices. No person can choose for us; we determine our destiny. Zen has affirmed with great imagination that real life is open, receptive, responsive, and spontaneous. This is especially reflected in the everyday experiences of eating, working, sharing, and meditative listening.

Since the Way believes this Divine-Human Encounter to be the deepest clue to life, it is not surprising that others have also discerned various aspects of it. It would be more surprising if others were totally oblivious of this drama. Again we find that what seems most unique in the vision of the Way turns out to be also most universal in its understanding and expression.

THE DIVINELY INTENDED TENSION

The theme of the Way could well be the title of one of Margaret Mead's anthropology books: *New Lives for Old*. The Community of the Resurrection witnesses to the power that re-creates the new in the midst of a world where the old ways of stagnation and death are strongly operating.

The classic description of this basic understanding of the Way is expressed in the early missionary writings of St. Paul: "Therefore, if anyone is in Christ, he is a new creation; the old has passed away, behold, the new has come. All this is from God, who through Christ reconciled us to himself and gave us the ministry of reconciliation" (2 Cor. 5:17–18).

The Way constantly uses the word "new." It believes that a new age has dawned; good news is available and must be shared in new ways; a new creation is taking place through a renewing power; the foundational scriptures are called the New Testament; people experience the new birth; the community is sometimes called the "New Israel." We have seen that the words using the prefix "re–" —redeem, revive, regenerate, repent—are used to describe the new life of the Way.

The Way lives from the Center, which is the source of the radical "breakthrough" of the new into the old life. It has happened and it continues to happen. Time before the knowledge of this central Christ-event is described as B.C.—Before Christ. Time lived in the realization of the light, life, love, and power of Jesus

Christ is called A.D.—*Anno Domini*, in the year of our Lord. Even secular history uses this rough classification. In our personal histories, it is possible to be living in A.D. 1980 but in a condition which is, for all practical purposes, lived B.C.—without direct contact with the re-creative power of Our Lord the Spirit. But once the closed-door existence passes away and the open-door existence begins, a "new creation" takes place. This new way of life is described by the Way as a life "in Christ." This means a life in the sphere where the renewing Spirit is operating and where there is openness to the renewing life. (This phrase "in Christ" is one of the most common in the New Testament; it is used over 150 times, largely in the writings of St. Paul.) In our personal history it is possible to pass from a basically B.C. to an increasingly A.D. existence!

But all of this, true as it is, may sound too grandiose and unrealistic. For in actual experience the new life is always found in the closest connection with the old life. What we here refer to as *the old life* is really the common, average, everyday life about us and in us. Daily life is a mixture of good and bad, sublime and ridiculous, a few steps forward and a few steps backward. We live with a generous mixture of struggle, aspiration, quests, defeats, and endless opportunities for the exercise of patience and couage. This average everydayness has been called "the still, sad music of humanity."

It is this ordinary life which the various Asian Paths have also described vividly and thoroughly. The pendulum swings widely between near despair and intense aspiration. The Buddha went to great lengths to describe the drift of common life toward old age, sickness, and death. He gave detailed psychological descriptions of the effects of greed, anger, and delusion. At times people have thought of him as unduly pessimistic. He would have thought of himself as necessarily realistic, even as a careful physician seriously considers the disease before attempting the cure. But basically he was optimistic. He believed there was a cure for the disease and a way of liberation for the enslaved. Hinduism, likewise, has vividly described the slavery of the treadmill existence. But then it goes on to point in the direction of enlightenment and emancipation.

The mixture of ordinary, universal life was accepted as "normal" until the *new life* appeared which makes all previous life look *old* by comparison. In fact, one of the most startling features of the new life of the Way is the emerging of the vivid sense of a new tension which had not existed before. The new produces a dynamic tension within the old life. Baron Friedrich von Hügel, the inspired lay Roman Catholic spiritual director of the last generation, used to call this the "Divinely Intended Tension."

This new tension is not a paralyzing tension. It is an intense sensitization, or heightened awareness, of new life growing in the midst of the old. The lotus is beginning to flower in the midst of the muck. But we are made simultaneously aware of *both* new *and* old! This is why a healthy-mindedness cannot stop with simply exulting in the new as if the old were no longer in existence. Followers of the Way always stand in need of the warning that was given to early members in the Epistle to the Ephesians: "Put off your old nature which belongs to your former manner of life and is corrupt through deceitful lusts, and be renewed in the spirit of your minds, and put on the new nature, created after the likeness of God in true righteousness and holiness" (Eph. 4:17–24). Followers of the Way pray steadily the Lord's Prayer: "Forgive us our sins, as we forgive those who sin against us." There is, then, a permanent and unrelaxed tension between the beginnings of the new life and the ever-present power of the clinging, old life.

St. Paul was acutely aware of this necessary creative tension as a key element of the new creation. This is one reason why his writings have been a source of inexhaustible vitality to subsequent generations. In fact, a revived life of the Way has usually come through a fresh discovery and application of the insights of this early missionary. He wrote: "But I say, walk by the Spirit, and do not gratify the desires of the flesh. For the desires of the flesh [old life] are against the Spirit [new life], and the desires of the Spirit are against the flesh; for these are opposed to each other, to prevent you from doing what you would. But if you are led by the Spirit you are not under the law. . . . And those who belong to Christ Jesus have crucified the flesh with its passions and desires. If we live by the Spirit, let us also walk by the Spirit" (Gal. 5:16–25).

Creative tension is a mark of the new life of the Way. There is always a sense that we are just beginning, or we are beginning all over again. We are future-oriented. We have been "sealed" or "stamped" by the Spirit (2 Cor. 1:22). This is, at best, a "pledge" or "downpayment" of a process in our lives and in all history which is just beginning to unfold (2 Cor. 5:5; Eph. 1:14). The signs of the break-through of the new are the "first fruits" of an eventual fruitful harvest

(Rom. 8:23). The most typical awareness of the followers of the Way is expressed in such words as: "We know that the whole creation has been groaning in travail together until now; and not only the creation, but we ourselves, who have the first-fruits of the Spirit groan inwardly" (Rom. 8:22–23). "But one thing I do, forgetting what lies behind and straining forward to what lies ahead, I press on toward the goal for the prize of the upward call of God in Christ Jesus" (Phil. 3:13, 14).

This means that followers of the Way are not giddy ecstatics, out of touch with the real struggles of the world. All of the old life we know, and we know it even more vividly and seriously because it is now seen in the light of the new. Far from achieving maturity, we are but beginners in the Way. The Way is not a tension-free existence. Rather it is marked by a heightening of the "Divinely Intended Tension." It is like the tightening of the violin strings, which is necessary for the production of beautiful music. Not the absence of tension, but the production of creative tension is a characteristic of the Way.

FROM MYTH TO MYTH-FACT

Whenever a Christian missionary preaches for the first time to a people who have never heard the Gospel, he makes the amazing discovery that God has already been long at work in the situation, preparing the people for the coming of the Gospel. This is a universal missionary experience; it has been so from the first days of the preaching of the Way. As St. Augustine said, "God places salt on our tongues so that we thirst for him." This was early spoken of as the "Preparation for the Gospel." This is found chiefly in the myths, ritual, worship, customs, and folk-wisdom of the people. After this amazing discovery Paul said, "God has nowhere left himself without witness" (Acts 14:17).

This was powerfully illustrated among the Karen Christians in Burma with whom I was fortunate to live for many years. Before the coming of the Christian missionaries the Karens lived in the mountains and the most remote spots of Burma as a discouraged people in a nearly hopeless condition. *Nearly* hopeless, but not wholly hopeless! Their imagination was nourished by the constant telling of a great myth. (Myth in this case means a Big Picture containing deep wisdom in imaginative form.) They claimed that originally they had been a great people who knew God, enjoyed life, and lived from the wisdom of "the Book." But they had grown careless and the book of wisdom had dropped through the bamboo floor down to the ground below the house where the animals lived. Then the book was lost. But, they kept repeating, a new day will come for them. A white brother will sail across the waters in a great boat and bring them the "Golden Book." When this happens they will once again find God and a new way of life, which will usher in a new chapter in their racial history. Missionaries were quick to build on this and say that the Bible contained the news and the power of a new life from God for the Karens. Today one of the great Christian communities in Asia is found among these remarkable people.

Something like this has happened again and again in the history of the Community of the Resurrection. The myths which have kindled the imaginations of the peoples have come to be seen as a special "Preparation for the Gospel." They are natural "points of contact" for the Christian message.

One myth has been nearly universal and so of special importance. This is the story of the dying-rising God. In almost every culture there has been some variation on this basic myth-theme. Through carelessness and disobedience the land has been cursed; all is sick and out of joint. But if the king, or his son or another representative, will pass through the darkness of death, there will then come new life to the world. The curse will be removed; spring will break forth and banish the bleakness of winter's death. Through a sacrificial death resurrection life will come to the world. This was often given ritual expression in New Year's or spring festivals.

In our time it is C. S. Lewis, the brilliant Oxford and Cambridge Professor of Renaissance Literature and refreshing lay theologian, who has taken this subject most seriously. He gave a life-time of scholarly study to the myth-making capacity and its importance for our lives. More than almost anybody in his generation he helped to "unfreeze the imagination" so that truth-through-pictures could once again play its rightful part in our lives. He was speaking to a generation that had nearly lost the ability to use "the feeling intellect."

In his early days, before he became a Christian, he was fascinated with the place of myth and ritual in the life of Norse and Celtic cultures. Here he discovered the importance of this dying-rising God theme. He kept wondering where and how this originated, how it spread, and just why this particular myth came to mean so much to so many people. He described himself as one "who first approached Christianity from a delighted interest in, and reverence for, the best pagan imagination, who loved Balder before Christ and Plato before St. Augustine."[3]

In time he began rather nervously to wonder if this really was a true picture, and if it described something that had really happened. His close friend at the time was J. R. R. Tolkien, author of *The Hobbit* and *The Lord of the Rings*. Tolkien was a believing, practicing Roman Catholic Christian who also had a serious interest in myths and their relationship to the Christian faith. Tolkien gently suggested that the myth of the dying-rising God *had actually happened* and this was what Christians meant by the incarnation and resurrection of Jesus Christ. In time C. S. Lewis found his old defenses against the Christian faith melting away. After a period he, too, became a Christian. Lewis brought to his life an abiding appreciation for the place of myth and imagination in human experience.

C. S. Lewis saw that the persistence of this major myth-theme was a part of God's gracious calling, or luring, of the world back to the true way of life. In his *Mere Christianity*, Lewis wrote: God "sent the human race what I call good dreams; I mean those queer stories scattered all through the heathen religions about a god who dies and comes to life again and, by his death, has somehow given new life to man."[4]

We need have no fear that to rejoice in these good dreams will destroy the uniqueness of the Gospel. Actually, it should have the opposite effect. It should be an encouragement and helpful confirmation of the Gospel. Lewis put it this way: "Christ is more than Balder, not less. We must not be ashamed of the mythical radiance resting on our theology. We must not be nervous about 'parallels' and 'pagan Christs'; they *ought* to be there—it would be a stumbling block if they weren't."[5] He wrote: "If my religion is erroneous then occurrences of similar motifs in pagan stories are, of course, instances of the same, or similar error. But if my religion is true, then these stories may well be a *preparatio evangelica*, a divine hinting in poetic and ritual form at the same central truth which was later focused and (so to speak) historicized in the Incarnation."[6]

This, of course, is the crux of the matter. In Jesus Christ, at a certain point in Roman history—under Pontius Pilate—there came a "focusing and historicizing" of the great myth in the happening which Christians call the incarnation of Jesus Christ as "the Word of God made flesh." This is seen as the crucial (the word means "cross") event at the center of the world and the turning point of history. From this time on there is B.C. and A.D. In Lewis' words, *"the myth became fact."* But in becoming fact it did not despise or dispense with myth. Lewis wrote:

> Now as myth transcends thought, Incarnation transcends myth. The heart of Christianity is a myth which is also a fact. The old myth of the Dying God, *without ceasing to be myth,* comes down from the heaven of legend and imagination to the earth of history. It *happens*—at a particular date, in a particular place, followed by definable historical consequences. We pass from a Balder or an Osiris, dying nobody knows where or when, to a historical Person crucified (it is all in order) *under Pontius Pilate.* By becoming fact it does not cease to be myth: that is the miracle. I suspect that men have sometimes derived more spiritual sustenance from myths they did not believe than from the religion they professed. To be truly Christian we must both assent to the historical fact and also receive the myth (fact though it has become) with the same imaginative

embrace which we accord to all myths. The one is hardly more necessary than the other.[7]

This may sound threatening to the more timid and less imaginative followers of the Way. This was especially so for a generation which has been so indoctrinated by the dogmas of a too narrowly restricted scientific outlook that it has nearly lost the capacity to understand truth through symbols, metaphors, ritual, imaginative stories, and parables. Myth for many had come to mean the fanciful and the untrue. But, in our time, thanks to the efforts of many, such as C. S. Lewis, Charles Williams, J. R. R. Tolkien, and others, a renewed understanding of myth is helping us to appreciate with fresh conviction both the Gospel and the various "Preparations for the Gospel."

Actually, this is the rebirth of an old insight which the Community of the Resurrection has known from the beginning. From its earliest days it has insisted that: *Grace completes but does not destroy nature.* Lewis wrote: "For this is the marriage of heaven and earth: Perfect myth and Perfect Fact: claiming not only our love and our obedience, but also our wonder and delight, addressed to the savage, the child, and the poet in each one of us no less than to the moralist, the scholar, and the philosopher."[8]

WALKING ON TWO LEGS

To learn to walk steadily on two legs is not easy! There are lurching efforts, discouragements, loss of balance, and frequent falls. But coordination can be achieved with encouragement, guidance, patience, and practice. It is so easy to take for granted our capacity for a brisk morning walk. How awkward it would be to go through life hopping, first on one leg then on the other!

It is something like this in understanding the Christian Way as both unique and universal. To hop on one foot, or stress only one theme, to the exclusion of the other, is awkward and ineffectual. The two legs, or themes, need to be coordinated to make possible an effective, poised, gracious movement. This poise and balance is no simple achievement; there seems to be a life-long tendency to lose balance and resort to hopping.

In the earliest missionary preaching of the Way, as recorded in the New Testament, we find both themes. The strongest accent, quite naturally, seems to be on the hearty testimony that the new age has dawned. God has acted decisively in Jesus Christ in a way that is unique and, in a sense, final. This is to stress the *uniqueness* of the Way.

Often this was stated in stark and abrupt contrast to all other existing Paths. In a time of persecution St. Peter could defend himself boldly by saying: "This [Jesus Christ] is the stone which was rejected by your builders, but which has become the head of the corner. And there is salvation in no one else, for there is no other name under heaven given among men by which we must be saved" (Acts 4:11–12). St. Paul could sharpen the contrast to the best known Paths of his time by writing: "For Jews demand signs and Greeks seek wisdom, but we preach Christ crucified, a stumbling block to Jews and folly to Gentiles, but to those who are called, both Jews and Greeks, Christ the power of God and the wisdom of God. For the foolishness of God is wiser than men, and the weakness of God is stronger than men" (1 Cor. 1:22–25). St. John has

Jesus saying: "I am the way, and the truth, and the life; no one comes to the Father, but by me" (John 14:6).

But there is another strain in the New Testament. This is found in the very same sources and from the mouths and pens of the same people who, on other occasions, speak of the Way as the completion or fulfillment of the best that is found in the other Paths. This note stresses the *universality* of the Way.

The Gospel of Matthew has Jesus saying: "Think not that I have come to abolish the law and the prophets; I have come not to abolish them but to fulfill them" (Matt. 5:17). The Epistle to the Hebrews devotes its great literary and symbolic skill to demonstrating that the Jewish heritage is not lost, but fulfilled in the Way of Jesus Christ. It begins with these words: "In many and various ways God spoke of old to our fathers by the prophets; but in these last days he has spoken to us by a Son, whom he appointed the heir of all things, through whom also he created the world" (Heb. 1:1, 2). Even the ancient system of blood sacrifices is understood with appreciation and Christ is seen as the fulfillment of the deepest meaning of both the priest and the sacrifices. "For if the sprinkling of defiled persons with the blood of goats and bulls and with the ashes of a heifer sanctifies for the purification of the flesh, *how much more* shall the blood of Christ, who through the eternal Spirit offered himself without blemish to God, purify your conscience from dead works to serve the living God" (Heb. 9:13–14).

The same St. Peter, who can speak with such stark contrast when in a defensive mood, speaks in a different accent when confronted with a different preaching situation. In the house of a sincere Roman religious seeker, Cornelius, St. Peter can say: "Truly I perceive that God shows no partiality, but in every nation anyone who fears him and does what is right is acceptable to him" (Acts 10:35).

St. Paul can see evidences of the work of God in the worship of the people at Lystra, saying that God "did not leave himself without witness" but has given understanding of his nature through the forces of creation (Acts 14:17). He sees the educated conscience of the Greeks to function much like the Law of the Jews (Romans 2:14).

The Gospel of John, so filled with vivid contrasts, is also the source for some of the deepest insights into the universality of the Way. It is the prologue to this Gospel which sees the Word, or *Logos,* to be at work in "the making of all things." The life which was in the Word, or Christ, was the "light of all men." This was "the true light which enlightens every man." It was this light and word which became flesh and dwelt among us in the incarnation of Jesus Christ (John 1:1–14).

Followers of the Way with a Jewish background found their heritage both challenged and affirmed. Jewish Christians continued to value the Law, be inspired by the prophets, and worship God by singing the Psalms. But they did it with the fresh perspective that Jesus Christ brought. Old ideas of the Messiah were criticized and refocused in the light of Jesus of Nazareth and the experience of the cross and the resurrection. But even when Jewish Christians were forced to break away from the Jewish setting there was always the sense of the Way being a fulfilling, not a destroying Way. They saw themselves as the "New Israel" (Gal. 6:16).

But when the Way moved out from the Jewish milieu into the wider Greek-speaking world new questions arose. If one was in the Way how would you evaluate, say, the best of the mystery religions and the best of Greek philosophy? It was not easy to do justice to *both* the uniqueness *and* the universality of the Way. Some converts, such as the lawyer Tertullian, so emphasized the uniqueness as to virtually despise the Greek heritage. He wrote: "Wretched Aristotle! who taught them dialectics, that art of building up and demolishing, so protean in statement, so productive in disputes; self-stultifying, since it is ever handling questions but never settling anything. . . . What is there in common between Athens and Jerusalem? What between the Academy and the Church? Away with all projects for a 'Stoic,' a 'Platonic,' or a 'dialectic' Christianity! After Christ Jesus we desire no subtle theories, no acute inquiries after the gospel."[9]

But other converts, such as Justin, whose memory we invoked in the first chapter, sought to stress both the uniqueness and the universality. The Truth *(Logos)* which came in Jesus the Christ was the opening of a new and greater Way. In one sense the *Logos* in Jesus Christ was incomparable. But in another sense it was an extension, correction, and amplification of the seeds of the *Logos*, graciously given before the time of Christ in the best of Greek religion and philosophy. Loyalty to the Way could lead to appreciation, not simply annihilation, of the best of the Greek heritage.

Seemingly, the whole Community of the Resurrection contained both themes, held together in a fruitful tension: The Way is both unique and universal. This creative tension was the walking on two legs not hopping on just one. But this tension was not preserved in a static formula. It was maintained by a living, flexible encounter and dialogues with the other Paths. Some people in some situations were especially given the task of stressing the uniqueness; other people in other situations sensed an equal call to stress the universality. Perhaps we might say that the youthful, exuberant thrust into a new missionary situation calls for the accent on the unique; the more sober, reflective attempt to do justice to a rich cultural heritage and the continuing life of the Way calls for the accent on the universal. But both are needed and each needs the other. The wholeness and harmony of the Chinese Yin-Yang seems appropriate here.

I recall with great appreciation my friendship with two of the senior statesmen of the Christian community in Burma: U Tha Din, the father, and U Hla Bu, his son. When I arrived in 1952 U Tha Din was an old man, living with his children on the edge of the campus of the Burman Theological Seminary, where he had taught comparative religion for many years. I would go and talk with him as a way of practicing my Burmese and, even more, catching something of his remarkable spirit. U Tha Din had grown up in Central Burma in a very traditional Buddhist village. He knew intimately the Theravada Buddhist Path. But at some point he had made contact with the followers of the Christian Way. I am not sure of all of the details that led to his conversion.

His decision was a costly one. Although Burmese Buddhists are, on the whole, a generous and tolerant people, his decision to become a Christian caused great consternation in his conservative village. After a time he was dismissed from the village and I saw the place where he constructed a small hut in which to live beyond the village limits. After becoming a Christian he continued to take a keen interest in the Buddhist heritage as well as his newly found faith. He became well-versed in the Scriptures and practices of Buddhism. Later he became a professor in the Seminary, where his courses in comparative religion were an important part of the training of future Christian leaders. He was skillful in debate, and always an evangelist at heart. Having paid a price for his Christian faith he was keenly aware of the differences between the Christian faith and the Buddhism of his ancestors. While knowing two faiths well, his accent was largely on the uniqueness of the Christian Way.

His son, Dr. U Hla Bu, was one of the most respected leaders of the Church in Burma in my early years. He was the first Burman to earn a Ph.D. degree. He was the first Burman to become president of Judson College. When this was later absorbed by the University of Rangoon, Dr. U Hla Bu served with distinction as head of the department of philosophy. He was chairman of the Burma Christian Council and represented Burma at many ecumenical conferences. Later he served as Visiting Professor of World Christianity at Union Theological Seminary in New York.

Dr. U Hla Bu helped to give guidance to the Church in Burma when his country passed from the days of British colonial rule to the newly won Burmese independence. This was a time of renewed cultural appreciation and a government-sponsored Buddhist revival. For U Hla Bu's generation it was necessary to think deeply about the relationship of the Christian Faith, not only to the Western colonial past, but to the rich heritage of Burmese Buddhism. He was no less zealous and committed than his father; but the context of obedience and the demands of his time were very different. While always having a vivid sense of the uniqueness of the Christian faith, U Hla Bu sensed, with prophetic urgency, the need to stress the universality of the Way.

The vitality and sensitivity of this father and son reveal what I mean by the Way walking on two legs, not hopping on one. Surely the nineteenth-century expression of the Christian mission called for a strong accent on the uniqueness of the Way. But in more recent years we have come to see that for effective forward movement, both legs are needed. The equally difficult and demanding task of seeing the Way as universal has been largely ignored. Our times call out, all over the world, for attention to be given to this side.

When we consider the Way, not only by itself but in relationship to the Asian Paths, the necessity for this poised, balanced walking on two legs becomes apparent. Hopping on one leg simply will not do.

NOTES

1. C. S. Lewis, *Mere Christianity* (New York: Macmillan, 1964, 1970), p. vii.
2. All biblical quotations are taken from the Revised Standard Version of the Bible, Thomas Nelson, New York.
3. C.S. Lewis, *God in the Dock: Essays on Theology and Ethics*, ed. Walter Hooper (Grand Rapids, Mich.: Eerdmans, 1970), p. 132.
4. Lewis, *Mere Christianity*, p. 39.

6

MODELS FOR
THE ENCOUNTER OF FAITHS

The Christian Way and the Asian Paths will increasingly encounter each other and at greater depth. It is important to realize that certain models for the encounter are already in use. Some may be outmoded, or in need of reconditioning. Likely new models will need to be constructed. But it will help in facing the future to be aware of some of the presently operating models in the encounter of faiths.

THE DUNGEON

One of the oldest and the most persistent models for the relationship of the Christian Way to other Paths is the blunt, straightforward dungeon attitude. According to this point of view those who have not come into the light and the emancipating Good News of Jesus Christ are locked in a dark, cramping dungeon. The message of the Christ is the news of the possibility of light and freedom for all who hear and allow themselves to be saved from their present dungeon existence.

Of course the dungeon will seem like "home" to those who prefer this way of life. The dungeon can be elaborately decorated, showing the marks of culture and education; it may include an extensive library. The dungeon allows for some mental and physical exercises: various forms of meditation and religious disciplines can be practiced and even mastered while living in the dungeon. These religions of the dungeon, including the perversions of the Christian Way, can all be seen as attempts to "save oneself, by oneself." The religions of the dungeon are the monotonous efforts of self-realization. But none of these valiant and well-meant efforts are sufficient to really free oneself from the dungeon.

However, through Jesus Christ, as Light and Lord, the power to rescue all who will be rescued has come as a grace and a gift.

It is not strange that this appeal has a long history and is still widely influential in the thinking about the Christian mission in our time. It speaks to our deepest sense of need for more light and more freedom. Who is there with no sense of darkness and slavery! Who does not yearn to see more and become more! It also rightly senses the futility of much lift-yourself-by-your-own-bootstrap-salvation. It *sees through* "religion," even the "Christian *religion*." "Religion" easily gives false encouragement to complacency or pride: it reduces life to superficiality by an overly simple set of rules and empty cliches; or it fosters by a "misty mysticism" the illusion of some *deep* feeling of union with some would-be creative current of divine life. Likely self-deception is easiest in just this area. But the Gospel, according to the dungeon perspective, is a way of salvation *from* all religious legalism and mysticism.

The dungeon viewpoint is responsible for many of the Christian churches now found in Asia, Africa, and Latin America, as well as in the West. This point of view is found among Fundamentalists, Conservative Evangelical Protestants, and it has operated in many parts of the Roman Catholic Church. It cannot be read-off as "hopelessly nineteenth century!" It is strongly with us and in various forms will probably increase, not disappear. There are obvious strengths in this position. It is clear-cut and you can know where you stand when confronting it.

But, while recognizing its strengths, it is also necessary to note its weaknesses. It lends itself easily to authoritarian, dogmatic people whose style of relating to other people will almost always be on the basis of "*my* superior truth" and "*your* inferior error." (I'm OK; you're NOT OK.) The degree to which this immediately repels those who are outside this overly simple scheme is well-known to any "outsiders," but is seldom sensed by the "insider." Perhaps these "insiders" are also in a dungeon of their own; though this thought seems never to have seriously engaged them. Their need to approach others as "the lost" while they see themselves as securely among "the saved" may be evidence of a psychological condition to which the Christ seeks to come as corrector and healer, *not* encourager and condoner.

THE ROUND TABLE

At the opposite extreme from the dungeon is the round table. Here all are equals; there is no "head" at this table. This is the approach of the genial, tolerant, urbane, scholarly "Parliament of Religions." All are encouraged to bring into the searching discussions the best they have discovered. By earnest sharing, careful listening, and honest comparison all will be enriched; no one will be intimidated. No one has all the truth; each needs to hear the other.

This has great appeal, especially to those who have suffered from the blight of narrow-minded, imprisoning religion. The need to listen and learn from the sincere followers of other paths would seem to be obvious. Surely if we have any security in our own view we have nothing to lose by the novelty or challenge of another point of view. Having the need to always extend our perspectives, the value of the round table would seem to be assured.

Perhaps the round table is valuable if it is not accepted as the *only* piece of furniture in the home. Along with the round table (and its endlessly open discussions) there also needs to be the "hearth," where more life is shared than just "heady discussions." Also many will sense the need for some kind of "altar," where commitments are made; where adoration, repentance, and intercession are in order. This larger inclusiveness of furniture might save the round table from turning the Path into just another topic for scholarly discussion and endless detached speculation.

But the round table must also be watched for hidden agendas which get smuggled into the discussions. It would be wrong to use the round table as a gimmick to get people supposedly to discuss freely, when actually the management was trying to use this as a means to "convert" others to its own point of view. In this case a better dialogue would take place if all were "above board" about their intentions. For instance, it may be that the hidden presupposition of the round table is that all religions are basically the same, all are simply variations on a single theme. If this is assumed then this itself needs to be stated; because this is already a "faith stance," an attitude brought to the facts, not necessarily derived from them. If this can be discussed as one possible "faith stance" all may profit from the discussion. But if this is assumed to be "the Truth," which it is hoped that the slow and benighted will eventually embrace, the chances for significant dialogue are slight indeed.

GRADUATION FROM THE RELIGIOUS TO THE SCIENTIFIC STAGE

The influential perspective of this "graduation" is equidistant from either the dungeon or the round table. In a sense it is not so much a model for the encounter of faiths as it is an attitude which any thinking person must take seriously.

From this perspective all religions, including the Way and the Asian Paths, are part of the venerable legacy of the past. These religions have played their part in giving world views, comforting people in suffering, and binding people together in workable societies. But with the increase in critical thinking, especially with the rapid advance of scientific thinking, it is no longer possible (it is even retrogressive) to be stuck in an outmoded earlier stage. We *must* move from the kindergarten to the high school, and eventually to the university! Religion was important for the childhood of the race; now science will enable us to live as fully responsible adults in a world we can and must manage by our own intelligence.

An early, forceful spokesman for this point of view

was Auguste Comte (1798–1857), the founder of the modern academic discipline of sociology. He wrote of the "Law of the Three States." We are meant, he wrote, to pass through these stages: (1) the theological, or fictitious state; (2) the metaphysical, or abstract state; (3) the scientific, or positive state. The application of the critical point of view was a second or mediating state to help lead from the childhood of religion to the maturity of science. But, for Comte, science could provide a kind of new, advanced religion which he called "The Religion of Humanity." Under the organization of the scientific perspective the best of the past could be preserved. All would be taught to value "living for others." The term "altruism" was introduced by Comte.

There are many variations on this point of view. Communism thinks of itself as an applied scientific sociology and has encouraged the *withering away* of religions. Religions have a way of fostering other-worldly hopes, which allow people to succumb to social injustice when they should be engaged in revolutionary struggle for more social justice.

Certain forms of psychology, also, have urged and worked for the disappearance of religion which, they feel, adds a load of unnecessary guilt as well as enslaving one to outmoded, personality-damaging ideas.

Anyone concerned with the Way or the Asian Paths will have to seriously listen to this "secular" and "scientific" point of view. To fail to hear what these are saying would be to cut ourselves off from vast numbers of our generation to which this point of view has come as liberating good news. Also, many of the criticisms of childish religion and religion as a "drugging opium" contain truth that needs to be appropriated.

But perhaps the strength of this viewpoint is as a purifying fire, rather than as a satisfying "last word." Seemingly, we do not live by science alone, or criticism alone. We do need "metaphors," whole visions, over-arching myths, symbol systems, and these imply ritu-als, in order to relate to the whole scheme of things and to each other in significant depth. The inability of a limited scientific viewpoint to meet the larger and deeper needs of the human seems also to be a fact of experience that we must take into account. The whole fresh concern for religion among the present Western, scientific youth generation should not be dismissed as simply a "failure of nerve," or a reversion to a primitive stage. It may be another indication of the fact that the pendulum swings endlessly between "The Yogi and the Commissar." Both have a limited, but not a final perspective.[1]

Religions may be outmoded. But the "religious di-mension," meaning the capacity for wonder, worship, self-criticism, and inter-relatedness, seems constitu-tionally part of the human, perhaps a Spirit-created part. If so, to imply a "graduation" from the religious to the scientific may be simply a contemporary illusion fostered by accepting the "myth of science" too naively and uncritically.

THE HIGHER SYNTHESIS

The most prevalent mood among the more intellec-tual who ponder the encounter of faiths is in the direc-tion of a coming, higher synthesis; a more inclusive merging of faiths that will result in something newer and better.

"How many centuries is it," Andre Malraux has asked, "since a great religion shook the world."[2] But the static condition of the patchwork quilt cannot continue in our rapidly shrinking world. The new mingling of faiths will cause a fresh interpenetration of ideas and customs. Out of the encounter some paring of outmoded encrustations will perhaps take place. The new intercourse will fructify in more inclusive, universal faiths, perhaps even a new world faith as a basis for the coming world civilization.

The names and blueprints of many of the modern intellectual giants express and encourage this mood of hope for the coming, new, higher synthesis. Arnold Toynbee, in his *An Historian's Approach to Religion* and *Christianity among the Religions of the World*, sees the Paths divided between the Judaic (Judaism, Christianity, and Islam) and the Buddaic (Hinduism, Buddhism, and Taoism). The most important understanding to emerge from all of these Paths is the sense of suffering love as the highest value; hence, the key to God's nature and human action. This is to be found supremely in Mahayana Buddhism and Christianity. The future will see an accentuation of this. But, unfortunately, the Judaic group has always been cursed with a narrow-minded sense of being the chosen people, with a unique incarnation, and a special mission. If this excessively dogmatic viewpoint could be purged, and a more universalistic approach could be fostered, some higher synthesis of the best of both worlds will emerge.

F. S. C. Northrop, of Yale University, in his comprehensive work *The Meeting of East and West* has described the necessary philosophical basis for the emerging unification of East and West. The special contribution of the West has been in the area of analysis, science, and technology; the East has been strongest in intuition, art, religion, and wholeness. Either alone is incomplete. The future will see the union of the complementary opposites in a spirit much as the wise Chinese have harmonized the Yang and Yin, male and female, light and darkness, summer and winter. In Northrop's opinion the East has already welcomed the science of the West. It is now time for the West to welcome the intuitive, religious inclusiveness of the East. Religiously, he believes, the East has nothing to learn from the West; it is high time for the West to learn, religiously, from the East.

W. E. Hocking, of Harvard University, has contributed to this mood in his *The Coming World Civilization*. He credits Christianity with making possible, in the past, the conditions in which science could grow. Now this scientific approach is the actual unifying factor in the emerging world civilization. But to continue the vitality of the coming civilization the religious base will need to be a purged, expanded Christianity; something vastly changed from the present rigid, parochial religion we have known. His hopes for a "reconception" of Christianity would eliminate the doctrine of the "One Way" and focus on the common element which unites all the Paths: the sense of Being and Blessedness which the mystics of all faiths have found and to which they have witnessed. Differences in the Paths are incidental: they can be accepted for a while with tolerance, then slowly overcome as the mystical, common core of all faiths is accentuated.

Prophetic voices like these stretch our sluggish imaginations and cause us to think in larger, global terms. They nourish a hope of something vaster and more comprehensive than we have yet seen. For this reason their messages must be pondered.

At the same time it is necessary to recognize that these are largely the blueprints of brilliant individuals, emanating from the libraries of great Western universities. Patterns of great ideas can be handled more easily than the stubborn, unpredictable turns of history. Life-history is never as neat and pliable as the schemes would seem to make it. Often those elements which do not enter the schemes at all turn out to be the most determining events. Each of these thinkers, and this seems to be typical of the trend toward the higher synthesis, has the strengths and limitations of the spectator-attitude of the philosopher or cultural anthropologist. Less than justice is done to the Judaeo-Christian sense of history as the sphere of the concrete, unique and unpredictable. Much of the stubborn, raw-stuff of persons in unpredictable encounter cannot be dealt with in these schemes. Furthermore, it appears to be characteristic of the exponents of the higher synthesis that they are largely Western protagonists of "the superiority of the East."

It is necessary to hear, but also to keep probing these panaceas.

CHRIST, THE CROWN OF . . .

In 1913 J. N. Farquhar, a gifted Y.M.C.A. secretary in India, wrote a book called *The Crown of Hinduism*. This volume had a profound effect on Christian missionary thinking in that country. In many ways this model of the encounter of faiths is the dominant one among the largest number of Christians today.

Farquhar was deeply immersed in Indian life; he

had a profound respect for both Indian people and
Hinduism. He was concerned that the Christian mission in his time do full justice to both its Lord and the
Gospel, and also to the rich heritage of Indian spirituality and culture. Through a careful and sympathetic
study of Hinduism he discerned those aspects which
he felt to be Spirit-taught and which pointed beyond
themselves to some possible fuller understanding.

He believed that the Christ was "The Crown of Hinduism." In this unveiling of the mystery and meaning
of life through Jesus the Christ there was the summa-
tion and crystalization of the highest insights and richest tendencies of Hinduism. Seeing the Christ in the
light of the Hindu upreach in no way diminished his
greatness or uniqueness. Rather, it showed him as
related, in challenge, clarification, and consummation
to one of the religiously most gifted peoples of the
world.

Christ as "The Crown of Hindusim" was, again, a
creative "Middle Way" between the extremes of the
dungeon and the round table. Christ came to fulfill,
not to destroy, the best of Hinduism; but his coming
added a new dimension, not to be found apart from
him. Seeing Christ as "The Crown"—of whatever Path
was sympathetically investigated—was a way of doing
justice to both the uniqueness and the universality of
the Way. To take this approach seriously was a call to a
sympathetic and patient love of the people and their
Paths (albeit a critical, not a sentimental appreciation);
at the same time, it was a call to fidelity to the task of
sharing the life which the Christ has made available in
the world. This "double-faithfulness" was not so much
missionary schizophrenia as the wholeness which sees

life, with nuances and proportion, from the perspective of the fullest disclosure of the divine life. Here it is not a case of leveling down to the lowest common denominator, but leveling up to the highest possible revelation.

This model came with freshness in its day; in fact, to many it seemed very radical. This was because most Roman Catholic and Protestant missions were operating from some version of the dungeon model. Actually, however, it was radical in the best sense of that word—going to the root, or center. This is what the main, or classic, stream of the Christian Community had said, at its thoughtful best. Today some version of the "Christ, the Crown of . . ." model would be the approach of most Roman Catholics and most classical or liberal Protestants. For this reason it especially needs to be appreciated and criticized.

The *Documents of Vatican II* are important as an indication of the largest consensus of Roman Catholic thinking on current issues. These Documents tell more than some brilliant conjecture of a "far out" individual. They may be taken as the official thinking of the largest single body of Christians on this subject. In the "Declaration on the Relationship of the Church to Non-Christian Religions" it is stated:

> From ancient times down to the present, there has existed among diverse peoples a certain perception of that hidden power which hovers over the course of things and over the events of human life; at times. indeed, recognition can be found of a Supreme Divinity and of a Supreme Father too. Such a perception and such a recognition instill the lives of these peoples with a profound religious sense. Religions bound up with cultural advancement have struggled to reply to

these same questions with more refined concepts and in more highly developed language.

Thus in Hinduism men contemplate the divine mystery and express it through an unspent fruitfulness of myth and through searching, philosophical inquiry. They seek release from the anguish of our condition through ascetical practices or deep meditation or a loving, trusting flight toward God.

Buddhism in its multiple forms acknowledges the radical insufficiency of this shifting world. It teaches a path by which men, in a devout and confident spirit, can either reach a state of absolute freedom or attain supreme enlightenment by their own efforts or by higher assistance.

Likewise, other religions to be found everywhere strive variously to answer the restless searchings of the human heart by proposing "ways," which consist of teachings, rules of life, and sacred ceremonies.

The Catholic Church rejects nothing which is true and holy in these religions. She looks with sincere respect upon those ways of conduct and of life, those rules and teachings which, though differing in many particulars from what she holds and sets forth, nevertheless often reflect a ray of that Truth which enlightens all men. Indeed, she proclaims and must ever proclaim Christ, "the way, the truth and the life" (John 14:6), in whom men find the fullness of religious life, and in whom God has reconciled all things to Himself (cf. Cor. 5:18–19).

The Church therefore has this exhortation for her sons: prudently and lovingly, through dialogue and collaboration with the followers of other religions, and in witness of Christian faith and life, acknowledge, preserve, and promote the spiritual and moral goods found among these men, as well as the values in their society and culture.[3]

The footnotes to this section are also of importance in understanding this model of relationships. For instance, regarding "the exhortation for her sons" it states: "The Declaration gives a good example of prudence in putting aside, for the moment, elements in non-Christian religions that are repugnant to Christians (idolatry, etc.) to focus on the spiritual and moral *goods*. Also, there is here no undignified breastbeating, no protestation that Catholics were not responsible for unfortunate episodes in history, no exaggerated emotionalism—all of which would not have provided a good basis for persevering in dialogue."[4]

Regarding the claim that the Catholic Church rejects nothing which is true and holy in these paths the footnote significantly reads: "This paragraph presents an understanding that is traditional in the Catholic Church. One recalls, for example, Justin Martyr in the early Church attributing all the truths in non-Christian religions to the Word of God who enlightens every man who enters into this world—a concept found at the beginning of the Gospel according to John. Through the centuries, however, missionaries often adopted the attitude that non-Christian religions were simply the work of Satan and the missionaries' task was to convert from error to knowledge of the truth. This Declaration marks an authoritative change in approach. Now, for the first time, there is recognition of other religions as entities with which the Church can and should enter into dialogue."[5]

Protestantism, in general, has been strongest on the "either-or," emphasizing the uniqueness of the Way in contrast to all attempts at self-salvation. The "Catholic" emphasis has always attempted to preserve a "both-and" approach aiming at the universality of the Way, but not sacrificing the uniqueness.

With all due appreciation for the present rough consensus on this model, it is not without possible perils. Preserving the delicate balance of "Christ the Crown of . . . " may lead to a static acceptance of the Way and the Path without much dynamic interaction. It may, in short, be a formula leading nowhere. At the same time, one must be prepared for the fact that most Hindus and Buddhists will see it as only a slightly more sophisticated form of the old religious imperialism: Christ always ends on top, completing their inferior faith! Sometimes this is rejected as being an even more odious model than the "more honest" dungeon approach, which at least lets you know where you stand and does not gloss over the differences with loads of adjectives!

SOME SIGNIFICANT VOICES

Along with these models for the encounter of faiths there are some significant individual voices which need to be heard by followers of the Way in this time. Any building for the future should at least give serious attention to the labors of these stalwarts of the frontier.

Karl Barth

This hearty Swiss Protestant theologian had made every effort to view the human scene from the perspective of the gracious God who has come and keeps coming to us in Jesus Christ. He is suspicious of all attempts to use the frail vessels of human cultural achievements as ladders to try to reach up to an understanding of God and life. Nothing is to be gained by trying to climb a rope of sand!

In his *Church Dogmatics,* Vol. I, Pt. II, he speaks of "the Revelation of God as the Abolition of Religion." The history of human religion is, at best, a very "mixed bag." The Christian religion contains all the mixture of greatness and misery which can be found in other religions. High heroism exists side by side with fanaticism, superstition, and hypocrisy. Religion is the final stronghold where the human seeks to fashion its own security—only to discover that the fig leaves cannot cover the nakedness. God's dealing with us in Christ is not to make us more religious; but, if anything, to save us from religious phoniness. Religion, to Barth, is an expression of unbelief, or flight from the true God.

But once this is seen Barth goes on to recognize that the followers of the Way cannot escape enclosing their life style and beliefs in religious forms. This should make us patient, even understanding, of similar forms in other religions. But God accepts this Christian religion in forgiveness, even as he accepts sinners with a gracious welcome. God can use this Christian religion in his service, even as he makes use of forgiven sinners in his on-going ministry of reconciliation. Once this is seen there will be no glorying in the Christian *religion,* as such; and no time wasted in comparing the Christian *religion* with other religions, as if to show some special superiority of this religion. This would be tantamount to a careful comparison of my sins with your sins, which would be neither interesting nor instructive.

To live "by the grace of Christ," or in the power of

"the name of Christ," is to be freed from navel-gazing, religious introspection; from measuring ourselves and others with puny foot-rulers; and from trying to outdo others with our latest new clothing. It is to be at the disposal of God and others as a hearty friend, serving in joyous self-abandon in the common pursuits of life.

Paul Tillich

Paul Tillich's genius is for building careful bridges of understanding. He has sought to mediate and make connections rather than reveal abrupt contrasts like Karl Barth.

In his *Christianity and the Encounter of the World Religions* he has shown a method of seeing "religious depth" or aspiration in contemporary political and cultural movements. Communism, with its quest for a more just society, and scientific humanism, with its pursuit of truth and its application of science to human concerns, must be taken seriously by followers of the Way.

In a similar manner Christians must explore with patient understanding whatever affinities exist between, say, Christianity and Buddhism. The key themes of "The Kingdom of God" and "Nirvana" will be seen as occupying a similar place in each of the two faiths. It will then be important to investigate how each of these influences the peoples and nations affected by them in the concrete historical crises of our time.

This leads Tillich to affirm that in the present situation followers of the Way must give "dialogue" with other faiths the highest priority. "Not conversion, but dialogue. It would be a tremendous step forward if Christianity were to accept this! It would mean that Christianity would judge itself when it judges the others in the present encounter of the world religions."[6]

Tillich does not see or hope for a superficial mixture of religions or the victory of one religion over the others. "A mixture of religion destroys in each of them the concreteness which gives it its dynamic power. The victory of *one* religion would impose a particular religious answer on all other particular answers."[7] There is no point to relinquishing "one's religious tradition for the sake of a universal concept which would be nothing but a concept. The way is to penetrate into the depth of one's own religion, in devotion, thought, and action. In the depth of every living religion, there is a point at which the religion itself loses its importance, and that to which it points breaks through its particularity, elevating it to spiritual freedom and with it to a vision of the spiritual presence in other expressions of the ultimate meaning of man's existence. This is what Christianity must see in the present encounter of the world religions."[8]

Karl Rahner

The most distinguished Roman Catholic theologian in recent times is Karl Rahner. Drawing on the long Catholic tradition of "both-and," he has faced squarely the fact that so-called "non-Christians" are always subjects of the saving grace of the Holy Spirit. "It would be wrong to regard the pagan as someone who has not yet been touched in any way by God's grace and truth. If, however, he has experienced the grace of God . . . then he has already been given revelation in a true sense even before he has been affected by missionary preaching from without."[9]

Followers of the Way should relate to all of these God-loved, or already-graced, ones as if they were "anonymous Christians." This does not in any way dispense with the glad missionary task of sharing the knowledge and power of God which is made available through the Christ. But it means that it will be done as to one already related, and not to a total stranger or an "outsider." But even when the explicit message of the Christ is not understood or accepted, the positive relationship persists.

Rahner believes that the visible Christian Community may shrink in size and religious pluralism, even opposition to official Christianity, may very well increase in the coming days. Even so, "The Church will not so much regard herself today as the exclusive community of those who have a claim to salvation but rather as the historically tangible vanguard and the historically and socially constituted explicit expression of what the Christian hopes is present as a hidden reality even outside the visible Church."[10]

The *avant-garde people* (a refreshing way to view the Way, rather than a collection of *yesterday's people!*) will then witness and work joyfully in the face of much misunderstanding and even opposition. They will sense their mission in living among those who for many reasons feel compelled to reject institutional Christianity, but who in their own ways are caught up in "God's universal salvific will." "In other words, the others who oppose her are merely those who have not yet recognized what they nevertheless really already are (or can be) even when, on the surface of existence, they are in opposition; they are already anonymous Christians, and the Church is not the communion of those who possess God's grace as opposed to those who lack it, but is the communion of those who can explicitly confess what they *and* the others hope to be."[11]

This would be a refreshingly freeing way to continue the on-going Christian mission. Rahner concludes: "The Church will go out to meet the non-Christian of tomorrow with the attitude expressed by St. Paul when he said: What therefore you do not know and yet worship [and yet *worship*!] that I proclaim to you (Acts 17:23). On such a basis one can be tolerant, humble, and yet firm towards all non-Christian religions."[12]

NOTES

1. See the author's *The Yogi, the Commissar, and the Third-World Church* (Valley Forge, Pa.: Judson Press, 1972).

2. Andre Malraux, *Antimemoires*, trans. Terence Kilmartin (New York: Holt, Rinehart, 1968), p. 2.

3. Walter Abbott, ed., *The Documents of Vatican II* (New York: Guild Press, 1966), pp. 661–663.

4. Ibid., pp. 662–663.

5. Ibid., p. 662.

6. Paul J. Tillich, *Christianity and the Encounter of the World Religions* (New York: Columbia University Press, 1963), p. 95.

7. Ibid., p.96.

8. Ibid., p. 97.

9. Karl Rahner, *Theological Investigations*, Vol. 5 (Baltimore: Helicon, 1966, New York: Seabury), p. 131.

10. Ibid., p. 133.

11. Ibid., p. 134.

12. Ibid.

Suggestions for Further Reading

Barth, Karl. *Church Dogmatics*, Vol. I, Part 2. Edinburgh: T. and T. Clark, 1956, 1963; Naperville, Ill.: Allenson, 1969.

Cragg, Kenneth. *The Christian and Other Religions: The Message of Christ*. Providence, R.I.: Mowbray, 1977.

The Documents of Vatican II. Edited by Walter Abbott. New York: Guild Press, 1966.

Neill, Stephen, *Christian Faith and Other Faiths: The Christian Dialogue with Other Religions*. 2nd ed. London: Oxford, 1970.

Panikkar, Raymond. *The Unknown Christ of Hinduism*. London: Darton, Longman and Todd, 1964: Atlantic Highlands, N.J.; Humanities Press, 1968.

THE "PASSING OVER" AND THE "COMING BACK"

THE NEW FACT IN OUR TIMES

John Dunne, the Notre Dame theologian, has given a clear description of the new dimension to the encounter of faiths in our time. In his rich and wise book *The Way of All the Earth* he has described what he calls the "passing over" and the "coming back" as the most important religious fact of our times. He writes:

Is a religion coming to birth in our time? It could be that what seems to be occurring is a phenomenon we might call "passing over," passing over from one culture to another, from one way of life to another, from one religion to another. Passing over is a shifting of standpoint, a going over to the standpoint of another culture, another way of life, another religion. It is followed by an equal and opposite process we might call "coming back," coming back with new insight to one's own culture, one's own way of life, one's own religion. The holy man of our time, it seems, is not a figure like Gautama or Jesus or Mohammed, a man who could found a world religion, but a figure like

122

Gandhi, a man who passes over by sympathetic under-standing from his own religion to other religions and comes back again with new insight to his own. Passing over and coming back, it seems, is the spiritual adventure of our time. . . . The course such an adventure follows is that of an odyssey. It starts from the home-land of a man's own religion, goes through the won-derland of other religions, and ends in the homeland of his own. . . . One has to pass over, to shift standpoints, in order to enter into the life of Jesus, even if one is a Christian, and then one has to come back, to shift standpoints again, to return to one's own life. From this point of view all the religions, even one's own, become part of the wonderland in this odyssey. One's own life is finally the homeland.[1]

Growth always implies risk. There is no standing still; we either are growing or we are shriveling. But growth demands a going out; a "passing over" into a new experience, a new point of view, another's world. This carries the threat of being torn away from old moorings. But it can also be the way of enlargement, fresh perspective, deepened insight. If the "passing over" can become the occasion of enrichment then "coming back" will mean a changed, expanded, and more richly inclusive "home" from which to continue the odyssey.

This "passing over" is possible because being a per-son means that nothing human is alien to us. (*Homo sum: humani nil a me alienum puto.* Terence) John Dunne suggests, "Perhaps this is the wisdom and the bliss of the sage. It is a sense of his completeness as a human being, a realization that he has within himself every-thing any other person has, that he has all the richness and all the resources of humanity. If this is the wisdom of the sage, then it consists in an appropriately simple insight. It is so simple that it can seem to be no insight at all. It is simply the realization that he is a human being. It is simple, but not common."[2]

It has never been doubted that *in some measure* it is possible for all of us to participate in Moses' awe before the burning bush; Isaiah's call in the temple; Jeremiah's hesitancy at his sense of inadequacy; Mary's desire to be an instrument in the Lord's service; Jesus' temptations in the wilderness, and his endurance of the cross; Paul's sense of guidance by the Spirit as he sought to follow his path of obedience and missionary service; and Teresa's desire to express her devotion to her Lord in practical reforms of ailing institutions.

What many in our day are also finding is that being human is also the door of access to Gautama's coming to an end of himself in the well-tried paths and his expectant waiting beneath the Bo-tree; Krishna's call to serve in one's station without demanding "success"; Hui Neng's discovery that the kitchen chores need not preclude insight or peace, that meditation can be a source of strength and vision.

This capacity for "passing over," even into other "traditions of response to the *Logos*" (John Taylor), is the mark of our capacity for growth toward an enlarged wholeness. "Passing over, therefore, entering sympathetically into other lives and times, if we are on the right track, is the way to completeness. This is not an unlikely hypothesis. For whenever a man passes over to other lives or other times, he finds on coming back some aspect of his own life or times which corresponds to what he saw in others. Passing over has the effect of activating these otherwise dormant aspects of himself."[3]

THE ANALOGY OF FRIENDSHIP

The "passing over" to another faith is analogous to the risks and rewards of friendship. Even as saints and crucial figures of a religion become the doors for entering into new understandings, so are friendships the "sacraments" (the earthly means of grace) which give us access to worlds other than our own.

I am writing these pages in the Library of Drew University in Madison, N.J. Some years ago this was my home. With my family we are enjoying a summer here visiting children, former neighbors and friends, before heading for a new missionary assignment in Hong Kong. Madison is a happy place for us, rich in memories and rich in friendships.

I am particularly thinking of friendships with some Italian Roman Catholics in this city. It is quite possible to live in Madison as a white Anglo-Saxon Protestant and have very little understanding of the other half of the city. But friendship becomes a door to a wholly different world.

I lived here during the sixties when Vatican II was bringing great, fresh stirrings to conservative, immigrant Roman Catholic communities. Friendships with some of these Italian Roman Catholics became a most enriching experience. In giving themselves they allowed entrance into another world. Immigrant struggles; second-generation immigrant sensitivities; a world of Roman Catholic piety—a mixture of Europe and America; so conservative on the one hand, and so responsive to change on the other; all of this would have been an impenetrable other-world until friendship opened the door.

To "pass over" is to enter a new world; to "come back" is to return a different person. One is bound to look at one's own world with fresh eyes and with fresh questions once the journey of friendship has been taken.

As I think of it, this *does* seem to be the way it has happened in my own experience; perhaps this is a clue to this new fact of "passing over" in our times.

Whatever understanding of Buddhism I acquired during the decade I lived in Burma largely came through the doors of significant friendships. I recall one of the first Burmese Buddhist families I came to know and love and whose friendship has been an enrichment now for over twenty years. These people opened their home and their hearts to a stranger, even with the dubious title "Missionary." They invited us on pilgrimages to pagodas, special celebrations during their holy days, family functions, and festival days; they shared the struggles of marriage, vocational crises, and death. This gave us access to a world where Theravada Buddhism is a living force, shaping the viewpoint of real people. Friendships like these were bridges to other worlds. To "pass over" meant to see with other eyes; to "come back" meant a heightened appreciation of both similarities and differences in the two worlds. The journey surely meant an expansion of understanding.

It is easy to see why a narrow, fearful, sect-mentality always urges a careful restriction of personal contacts. One can be "contaminated" by alien perspectives!

Friendships are risky and threatening adventures. They can draw us out of our isolation and our restricted worlds. They force new concerns, new questions, and new priorities upon us. If we want to "remain the same" it is best not to venture out in significant friendships!

But life behind the closed door is really the way of death. In our times the passion to "pass over," especially in the matter of the religious odyssey, has the potential of being a path to an open and enriching future. But this new fact must be well understood, wisely nourished, and carefully disciplined if it is to yield the fruits of an enriched integration.

THE MOUNTAIN WHERE THE WIND OF THE *TAO/LOGOS/CHRIST* BLOWS

In friendship both persons are apt to be changed; but the ways and degrees of change cannot be programed or predicted. There is a mystery and a risk in self-giving. We can be hurt or be enriched in the process; but there is no future in being calculating or manipulative. It is only by our willingness to give ourselves that we make possible the other's self-giving, which becomes the source of our enrichment. In all of life, but supremely in friendship, only those who risk losing life will find it; the resurrection follows the costly cross.

This law of life applies both in the "passing over" into other lives and also in "passing over" into what John V. Taylor has well called other "traditions of response to the *Logos.*" He states in his recent *The Go-Between God: The Holy Spirit and the Christian Mission:* "The eternal Spirit has been at work in all ages and all cultures making men aware and evoking their response, and always the one to whom he was pointing and bearing witness was the Logos, the Lamb slain before the foundation of the world. Every religion has been a tradition of response to him, however darkly it groped towards him, however anxiously it shied away from him."[4]

To "pass over" in a sympathetic desire to understand the other's "tradition of response" may change me; and in time it may help to modify the other tradition. But this, no more than in friendship, can be predicted or controlled. There is a mystery in the meeting. But of this there can be no doubt: The earnest "passing over" can be turned to my enrichment on my "coming back."

High on a mountainside in the New Territories of Hong Kong, overlooking an exquisitely beautiful coastline, stands an attractive octagonal chapel, looking very much like a Buddhist pagoda. This mountain, and the Christian community which forms the Institute located on it, is known as *Tao Fong Shan,* "The Mountain Where the Wind of the *Tao* (or *Logos,* or Christ) Blows." The symbol of this place is the cross rising out of the lotus. The highest of Asian and Buddhist wisdom is brought to touch, and in a sense culminates in, the symbol of the self-giving of the Christ-love. This unique place has sought to demonstrate, and so symbolize, the most sympathetic and sensitive encounter of faiths. At its best, its intent has been that sympathetic understanding of faiths which we have been describing as the "passing over" and the "coming back."

The inspiration behind this center of worship, study, and dialogue was the Norwegian Lutheran missionary, Karl Reichelt (1877–1952). This pathfinder was years ahead of his times; perhaps only now can we begin to see on a world scale the importance of the kind of dialogue he was seeking to foster in China.

He arrived in China in 1903 and early became concerned with the poor quality of contacts between Christians, especially Western missionaries, and the most sensitive Buddhist and Taoist monks and lay people. A visit to the famous Weishan Buddhist Monastery near Ninghsiang left an indelible impression on him. Later he wrote, "I got a glimpse of a peculiar and exclusive world, a world charged with deep religious mysticism, a world full of tragedy and heart-rending, but also marvellously rich in points of contact and sacred religious material." He felt a special call from the Spirit to prepare himself for a new kind of relationship and mission to these great people; "a special work, by the cultivation of friendly intercourse with the monks and the religious and enlightened lay people."⁵ From then on he gave himself to a sustained first-hand study of the life and practices of the best of Buddhism and Taoism in China.

In 1922 he had formed a small Christian brotherhood and established a new type of Christian "monastery" in Nanking. This became a place where visiting monks and serious "seekers" could come for meditation, classes, discussion, and contemplation. The Christian faith was presented in an atmosphere as conducive as possible to those with rootage in the *Tao*, as understood by both Buddhists and Taoists. In the process Christians also came to see Chinese religion and their own faith in deeper ways. During the early years the visiting monks averaged over a thousand a year.

From the first a few became Christians and were

baptized. But Reichelt was convinced that he must not exert any undue pressure in this direction. He also sensed that something deeper was going on in this interchange. He began to feel that perhaps the most significant work was that which was happening to those Buddhists who "passed over" for a time and then returned with fresh eyes to their old traditions. These were known as the "Friends of the *Tao*" who did much to modify the atmosphere of temples and monasteries in far-flung places. Reichelt wrote of them: "Although not joining the external church such enter the yearly increasing number of *unknown and unregistered Christ-followers.*"[6]

After the "Nanking Incident" of 1927 Reichelt moved his center to the present location in Hong Kong, which he hoped would be central for fruitful "passing over" and "coming back" for the whole great area of Southeast Asia. Here, with the help of a specialist in Chinese Buddhist architecture he built the Hall of Hospitality, the Christ Chapel, the library, lecture halls, residences, and dormitory. In describing the work of the Center he wrote:

> Here is our great aim: We wish everybody who comes up to this mountaintop and dwells in the buildings erected here may come under the unique, powerful, renewing spirit of Christ—that they may get that physical, mental, and spiritual blessing which emanates from the living and all-embracing spirit of Christ. Here we will welcome all religious people of whatever nationality and whatever religion, welcome them in the open-court of the universal, the cosmic, the all-embracing Saviour Jesus Christ. Here we wish that you all may feel at home in the *Logos* Wind that is blowing. Here we hope to get a resting place, a place for medita-

tion and holy fellowship, which may enable us to go out into God's wonderful world with a burning desire to serve humanity in love and wisdom.[7]

Reichelt called his approach "The Johannine approach";[8] he believed it to be in direct line with the prologue to the Gospel of John. Here was described God's Word, which in the Greek was *Logos* and was translated as *Tao* in the Chinese Bible, which was active in the creation of the world, and is continuously active as the "light that enlightens every person coming into the world." This *Logos* was reflected in the Light and *Tao* and *Dharma* of the Asian peoples and was the source of all that was true and good in their lives. To be sure, this *Logos* was rejected as well as accepted. Of the verse, "He came unto his own home and his own people received him not" (John 1:11) Reichelt said that this was the history of religions "in a nutshell." He believed his approach was in direct line with St. Paul's preaching to the Greeks on Mars Hill in Athens (Acts 17).

He was, of course, greatly misunderstood in his time. His own mission board recalled him and eventually it was necessary to form a new society to support the work. The symbol of the lotus and the cross appeared as "syncretism" (a phony mixture) to those who felt their main calling to be the straightforward conversion of the Chinese to "Christianity." Reichelt was always ready to explain that he considered his dialogical work to be missionary and evangelistic in the best sense. He once wrote in a letter: "Our work is therefore strictly Christo-centric, but consequently broad-minded."[9] He could agree with St. Augustine that "in all religions some truths are to be found. And these truths in all religions are really Christian truths, although the name of Christianity had not yet appeared." But the gleams and hints scattered throughout the religious world could be fully appreciated only in the light of the fullness of light and life in the *Logos*, or *Tao*, become flesh in Jesus Christ. It is the one who has seen the Incarnate Christ who can trace his footsteps elsewhere.

But for all of his protests that he was really an evangelist at heart, there was no disguising the fact that there was a different quality and impact in his approach. The intimacy of his knowledge of other paths and the depth and sincerity of his personal friendships meant that, in some sense, he had "passed over" into those "traditions of response" which he encountered. And his "coming back" had made him a different person—different in his relationship to Buddhists and Taoists, and different in his perceptions of his own Christian inheritance.

"The Mountain Where the Wind of the *Tao-Logos-Christ* blows" has been what Gandhi would call "an experiment with truth." Its checkered institutional history has been affected by mission-society politics, budgets, international wars, and changes in the political conditions of China. In many ways it has only partially fulfilled Reichelt's high hopes; in some ways its real impact, on a world scale, is just coming into its own. As for the Chinese Buddhists and Taoists, it can be seen that only a few—but some important individuals—have found the mountain to be a "bridge" to the Christian faith. Many more have found it a place of enrichment for their "coming back." For Christians it has probably not been a "bridge" to Buddhism or Taoism. But it began to be sensed (and this has been very threatening to some) that the mountain may cause one to "come back" a very different Christian! This need hardly be a surprise since this is the threatening-expanding experience of serious friendship.

In 1927 in a preface to Reichelt's *Truth and Tradition in Chinese Buddhism*, Logan Roots wrote: "We are learning that self-knowledge in the individual grows chiefly through intercourse with his fellows, and that the principle involved in this fact applies also to nations. I believe we can hardly fail to see from this study, even if we have not seen it before, that deeper knowledge of its own surpassing inheritance will come to Christianity from such intercourse as this book records and invites between itself and Buddhism."[10]

This mountain, then, with its octagonal Christ-Chapel and the symbol of the lotus and the cross may well be a symbol of the contemporary frontier in which the "passing over" and the "coming back" is "the spiritual adventure of our time."

THE TREASURE BENEATH OUR FLOOR

Martin Buber, the Jewish philosopher, has preserved for us a Hassidic parable which may well throw a flood of light upon our strange and adventurous times.[11]

The story concerns a Rabbi Eisik, son of Rabbi Jekel, who lived in the ghetto of Cracow, the capital of Poland. He had suffered numerous afflictions and was very poor; but he was a faithful servant of the Lord his God.

One night Rabbi Eisik dreamed that he was summoned to travel to far-off Prague, the capital of Bohemia, and there dig for a hidden treasure that was buried beneath the large bridge which led to the castle of the Bohemian king. At first the Rabbi ignored the dream, but after it recurred twice more he took courage and set off on the quest.

Rabbi Eisik reached the bridge but discovered that it was guarded day and night by Bohemian guards. He could only come daily, look over the bridge, watch the guards, and cautiously examine the soil. Eventually the captain of the guards enquired why he came daily and what his business was. Rabbi Eisik was straightforward and naive and reported his dream exactly to the guard, who responded with an uproarious and incredulous laugh.

"You poor old ignorant man," the captain said. "No sane person would trust such stupid dreams! Why if I were so stupid as to act on my dreams I would be today wandering aimlessly in Poland! Let me tell you the dream I had. I dreamed that I was summoned to go to Cracow and dig for treasure in the dirty corner behind the stove in the home of one Eisik son of Jekel! I suppose half of the men in Cracow are called Eisik and the other half are called Jekel! Wouldn't that be the most stupid thing to do in all the world!"

The Rabbi found the brusk, Christian officer a likeable and humorous man. After thanking him for his advice he hurried home, dug in the neglected corner of his home and unearthed the treasure which quickly put an end to all of his misery.

Likely the treasure which contains the more-than-abundant wisdom and power of God is very close to us.

We would not need to travel far to get it. It lies in our own hearth. But for some strange and inexplicable reason it seems necessary to go on a faithful journey to a distant country and encounter the voice of a person of another faith before we can discover the treasure beneath our own floor. To despise the journey or ignore the voice of the person of another faith may be the surest way to live in poverty, while a treasure is nearby.

In our times the journey out, the encounter with the strange but friendly guide, may be the way in which we discover the priceless treasure that resides in our own hearth.

NOTES

1. John S. Dunne, *The Way of All the Earth: Experiments in Truth and Religion* (New York: Macmillan, 1972), pp. ix–x.
2. Ibid., p. 230.
3. Ibid., p. 180.
4. John V. Taylor, *The Go-Between God: The Holy Spirit and the Christian Mission* (Philadelphia: Fortress Press, 1973), p. 191.
5. Quoted in Sverre Holth, "Karl Ludvig Reichelt, 1877–1952," *International Review of Mission* 41 (October 1952): 445.
6. Quoted in L. Noren, "The Life and Work of Karl Ludvig Reichelt," *Ching-Feng* 10 (1967): 18.
7. Ibid., p. 16.
8. Karl Reichelt, "The Johannine Approach," Madras Series, Vol. I (Authority of the Faith), p. 87.
9. Noren, "Life and Work," p. 28.

10. Karl Reichelt, *Truth and Tradition in Chinese Buddhism*, trans. Katrina Van Wagenen, 2nd ed. (New York: Paragon Book Reprint, 1969).

11. Found in Heinrich Zimmer, *Myths and Symbols in Indian Art and Civilization*, ed. Joseph Cambell, Bollingen Series, Vol. 6 (Princeton, N.J.: Princeton University Press, 1971), pp. 219–221.

Suggestions for Further Reading

Cobb, John B., Jr. *The Structure of Christian Existence.* Philadelphia: Westminster, 1967.

Dunne, John S. *The Way of All the Earth: Experiments in Truth and Religion.* New York: Macmillan, 1972.

Johnston, William. *The Still Point: Reflections on Zen and Christian Mysticism.* New York: Fordham University Press, 1970, 1977.

Newbigin, Leslie, *The Finality of Christ.* Richmond, Va.: John Knox Press, 1969.

Smith, Huston. *Forgotten Truth: The Primordial Tradition.* New York: Harper & Row, 1969.